Red Team Operations: Practical Approaches to Security Testing

Ritsu Shin'ya

Ritsu Shin'ya is a seasoned cybersecurity professional with over a decade of experience in the field. With a deep passion for security testing and red teaming, Ritsu has dedicated their career to understanding and mitigating the complexities of the cyber threat landscape. As a certified ethical hacker and penetration tester, they have worked with numerous organizations across various industries, helping them strengthen their security postures and safeguard their assets against ever-evolving threats.

Ritsu holds a degree in Computer Science and several industry-recognized certifications, including Certified Information Systems Security Professional (CISSP) and Offensive Security Certified Professional (OSCP). Their diverse background encompasses various aspects of cybersecurity, including vulnerability assessment, incident response, and security architecture.

In addition to hands-on experience, Ritsu is an avid researcher and educator, frequently sharing insights and knowledge through workshops, webinars, and articles in renowned cybersecurity publications. Their dedication to fostering a culture of security awareness and proactive defense is evident in every endeavor.

This book, "**Red Team Operations: Practical Approaches to Security Testing**," is a culmination of Ritsu's extensive experience and insights gained from years of red teaming engagements. It aims to provide practical approaches and methodologies to equip cybersecurity professionals, organizations, and security teams with the tools they need to navigate the complexities of modern threats.

Ritsu believes that effective red teaming is not just about breaking into systems but is a vital component of an organization's overall security strategy. By embracing the principles outlined in this book, readers can enhance their capabilities to think like an attacker, ultimately leading to more robust and resilient security programs.

Outside of work, Ritsu enjoys exploring new technologies, participating in cybersecurity competitions, and mentoring aspiring cybersecurity professionals. They are committed to sharing knowledge and building a community that prioritizes security in an increasingly interconnected world.

In an era where cyber threats are increasingly sophisticated and pervasive, the need for proactive security measures has never been more critical. Organizations face a myriad of challenges, from data breaches to ransomware attacks, and the consequences can be devastating. **"Red Team Operations: Practical Approaches to Security Testing"** serves as a comprehensive guide for cybersecurity professionals, organizations, and security teams looking to enhance their defenses through effective red teaming methodologies.

This book is designed to bridge the gap between theoretical knowledge and practical application, offering insights into the world of red team operations. Through a combination of proven techniques, real-world case studies, and actionable strategies, readers will gain a deeper understanding of how to think like an attacker and identify vulnerabilities before they can be exploited.

Each chapter delves into essential aspects of red teaming, providing a structured approach to security testing. From building a red team to understanding post-exploitation strategies, this book covers a wide range of topics that are critical for developing a robust security posture.

Chapter 1: Introduction to Red Teaming

This chapter sets the foundation by defining red teaming and its role within the cybersecurity ecosystem. It explores the differences between red, blue, and purple teams and highlights the significance of red team operations in enhancing organizational security.

Chapter 2: Understanding the Threat Landscape

Here, readers will examine current trends in cyber threats, common attack vectors, and notable case studies of major breaches. This chapter aims to provide context for the importance of red teaming in a rapidly evolving threat landscape.

Chapter 3: Building a Red Team

This chapter focuses on the essential skills and expertise needed to form an effective red team. It discusses team roles, responsibilities, and the importance of ongoing training and development to ensure team members remain at the forefront of cybersecurity practices.

Chapter 4: Red Team Methodologies and Frameworks

An overview of common frameworks used in red teaming, such as MITRE ATT&CK and NIST, is provided in this chapter. It also discusses how to select the right approach based on organizational needs and integrate red teaming into the overall security program.

Chapter 5: Planning and Scoping Red Team Engagements

This chapter addresses the critical aspects of planning red team engagements, including defining objectives, establishing legal and ethical considerations, and effectively communicating with stakeholders.

Chapter 6: Reconnaissance Techniques

Readers will learn about the various reconnaissance techniques used in red teaming, including passive and active reconnaissance, and how to gather open-source intelligence (OSINT) effectively.

Chapter 7: Exploitation Techniques

This chapter dives into the methodologies for discovering and exploiting vulnerabilities. It covers common exploitation techniques and tools used in the red teaming process, providing practical insights for effective testing.

Chapter 8: Post-Exploitation Strategies

After successful exploitation, this chapter explores strategies for maintaining access, data exfiltration, and clearing tracks. Understanding post-exploitation tactics is crucial for simulating real-world attacker behavior.

Chapter 9: Social Engineering Tactics

Social engineering is a powerful tool for red teams. This chapter discusses various social engineering techniques, the importance of conducting phishing simulations, and how to implement awareness training for employees.

Chapter 10: Physical Security Testing

This chapter highlights the significance of testing physical security controls. It provides techniques for assessing physical security measures and offers insights into how physical vulnerabilities can impact overall security.

Chapter 11: Reporting and Debriefing

Effective communication of findings is vital in red teaming. This chapter outlines how to structure reports, convey results to stakeholders, and conduct productive debriefing sessions to drive improvements.

Chapter 12: Lessons Learned and Continuous Improvement

This chapter emphasizes the importance of analyzing engagement outcomes and incorporating feedback into security practices. It discusses how organizations can evolve their red teaming approaches based on lessons learned.

Chapter 13: Tools of the Trade

An overview of essential tools for red teaming is provided in this chapter, comparing open-source and commercial options. It also covers setting up a red team lab for effective practice and experimentation.

Chapter 14: Real-World Red Team Engagements

Through case studies of successful red team operations, this chapter highlights common pitfalls and the impact of red teaming on enhancing an organization's security posture.

Chapter 15: The Future of Red Team Operations

In the concluding chapter, readers will explore emerging trends, the role of AI and automation in red teaming, and predictions for the future of cybersecurity, setting the stage for ongoing evolution in the field.

Chapter 1: Introduction to Red Teaming

In this opening chapter, we lay the groundwork for understanding the pivotal role of red teaming within the cybersecurity landscape. Red teaming, often seen as a simulated adversarial attack, goes beyond traditional penetration testing to provide a more holistic view of an organization's security posture. This chapter will define what red teaming entails, clarify the distinctions between red, blue, and purple teams, and explore the significance of these operations in today's threat environment. By examining the motivations behind red teaming and its historical context, readers will gain a solid foundation for the subsequent chapters, setting the stage for a deeper dive into the methodologies, techniques, and practical applications that will empower them to think like attackers and bolster their defenses effectively.

1.1 Defining Red Teaming

Red teaming has emerged as a critical component of modern cybersecurity strategies, enabling organizations to proactively assess their security posture and identify vulnerabilities before adversaries can exploit them. At its core, red teaming simulates real-world attack scenarios, providing organizations with a realistic assessment of their defenses and a better understanding of the tactics, techniques, and procedures (TTPs) used by malicious actors. This section will delve into the definition of red teaming, its key components, and its significance in the broader context of cybersecurity.

Understanding Red Teaming

Red teaming refers to the practice of employing a group of skilled security professionals, known as the red team, to mimic the actions of potential attackers. This team is tasked with identifying security weaknesses in an organization's systems, processes, and personnel through simulated attacks. Unlike traditional penetration testing, which often has a narrow focus and specific scope, red teaming takes a more holistic approach. It encompasses a wide range of attack vectors, including technical exploits, social engineering tactics, and physical security breaches.

The term "red team" originated in military strategy, where it referred to a group tasked with challenging an organization's strategies and plans by simulating enemy tactics. In cybersecurity, this concept has been adapted to create a structured methodology for assessing an organization's resilience against various cyber threats. The red team's goal is to think like an attacker, employing the same mindset and tactics that cybercriminals would use to infiltrate an organization.

Key Components of Red Teaming

Holistic Assessment: Red teaming goes beyond just testing the technical defenses of an organization. It evaluates the entire security posture, including physical security, personnel awareness, and incident response capabilities. This comprehensive approach enables organizations to identify weaknesses across various layers of their security infrastructure.

Realistic Attack Simulations: The red team's primary objective is to conduct realistic attack simulations that mirror the methods used by real-world adversaries. These simulations can include phishing attacks, social engineering, network exploitation, and physical intrusion attempts. By employing tactics that actual attackers might use, the red team can provide a more accurate assessment of an organization's vulnerabilities.

Adversarial Mindset: Red team members adopt an adversarial mindset, allowing them to think creatively and exploit security weaknesses in innovative ways. This mindset is essential for uncovering hidden vulnerabilities that may not be detected through traditional security assessments.

Collaboration with Blue Teams: Red teaming is most effective when there is a collaborative relationship between the red team (offensive) and the blue team (defensive). While the red team conducts simulations, the blue team monitors and responds to the attacks. This collaboration fosters a culture of learning, where both teams can share insights and improve their respective practices.

Reporting and Feedback: Following red team engagements, detailed reporting is crucial. These reports provide organizations with actionable insights and recommendations for remediation. The feedback loop created by sharing findings helps organizations prioritize security improvements and measure the effectiveness of their defenses.

The Importance of Red Teaming in Cybersecurity

The need for red teaming has become increasingly critical in the face of rising cyber threats and sophisticated attack vectors. Here are several reasons why red teaming is essential for organizations today:

Proactive Threat Identification: By simulating attacks before they occur, red teams help organizations identify vulnerabilities that could be exploited by real attackers. This proactive approach allows organizations to address weaknesses before they become the target of a successful attack.

Enhanced Security Awareness: Red teaming also serves to raise security awareness among employees. Through social engineering exercises, for example, organizations can educate their staff about potential threats and the importance of adhering to security protocols. This awareness helps create a culture of security within the organization.

Validation of Security Controls: Red teaming provides organizations with an opportunity to validate the effectiveness of their security controls. By testing defenses against real-world attack scenarios, organizations can assess whether their security measures are functioning as intended or if improvements are necessary.

Improved Incident Response: By conducting red team engagements, organizations can evaluate their incident response capabilities. Understanding how the blue team responds to simulated attacks can reveal strengths and weaknesses in incident response plans, enabling organizations to refine their procedures for actual incidents.

Regulatory Compliance: Many industries are subject to regulatory requirements related to cybersecurity. Red teaming can help organizations demonstrate compliance with these regulations by providing evidence of their proactive security testing efforts and ongoing improvements to their security posture.

Challenges in Red Teaming

While red teaming is a powerful tool for enhancing cybersecurity, it is not without its challenges. Organizations must navigate several potential hurdles to implement effective red team operations:

Scope and Boundaries: Defining the scope of a red team engagement is crucial to ensure that testing remains focused and effective. Organizations must clearly delineate which systems, processes, and personnel will be tested, and ensure that all stakeholders are aligned on the engagement's objectives.

Legal and Ethical Considerations: Red teaming can raise legal and ethical concerns, particularly when testing involves social engineering tactics or physical security breaches. Organizations must ensure they have the necessary permissions and adhere to legal frameworks to avoid liability.

Resource Allocation: Building and maintaining a red team requires resources, including skilled personnel, tools, and technologies. Organizations must allocate sufficient budget and staff to ensure the red team can operate effectively and provide meaningful insights.

Integration with Existing Security Practices: To maximize the value of red teaming, organizations must integrate these exercises into their existing security frameworks. This includes ensuring that findings from red team engagements are taken seriously and lead to actionable improvements.

Continuous Learning: Cyber threats are constantly evolving, and red teams must keep pace with emerging attack vectors and tactics. Organizations must prioritize continuous learning and skill development for their red team members to maintain effectiveness.

Red teaming is a crucial aspect of modern cybersecurity, providing organizations with a proactive means to assess their security posture and identify vulnerabilities before they can be exploited by real attackers. By simulating realistic attack scenarios and fostering collaboration between offensive and defensive teams, red teaming enables organizations to enhance their security measures, improve incident response capabilities, and promote a culture of security awareness. As cyber threats continue to evolve, the importance of red teaming will only grow, making it an indispensable component of a comprehensive security strategy. Organizations that embrace red teaming will be better equipped to navigate the complex landscape of cybersecurity, ultimately strengthening their defenses against an array of potential threats.

1.2 Roles in Cybersecurity

As cyber threats become increasingly sophisticated and prevalent, organizations recognize the critical need for diverse roles within their cybersecurity teams. Each role is designed to address specific aspects of cybersecurity, ensuring a comprehensive approach to safeguarding information and systems. This section will provide an overview of key roles in cybersecurity, highlighting their responsibilities, required skills, and the importance of collaboration among team members.

1.2.1 Security Analyst

Responsibilities: Security analysts are often the first line of defense in an organization's cybersecurity strategy. Their primary responsibilities include monitoring networks for security breaches, analyzing security incidents, and responding to alerts. They also conduct vulnerability assessments and implement security measures to protect sensitive information.

Required Skills:

- Proficiency in security tools and technologies (e.g., SIEM, IDS/IPS).
- Strong analytical and problem-solving skills.
- Knowledge of security protocols, policies, and best practices.
- Familiarity with programming languages and scripting (e.g., Python, Bash) can be beneficial.

Importance: Security analysts play a critical role in detecting and responding to security incidents, helping organizations mitigate risks and prevent breaches.

1.2.2 Security Engineer

Responsibilities: Security engineers design and implement security solutions to protect an organization's infrastructure. They work on configuring firewalls, intrusion detection systems, and encryption protocols. Additionally, security engineers may be involved in developing security architecture and ensuring compliance with industry standards and regulations.

Required Skills:

- In-depth understanding of network security and infrastructure.
- Experience with security tools and technologies.
- Strong knowledge of secure coding practices and application security.
- Proficiency in system administration and network protocols.

Importance: Security engineers are essential for creating robust security frameworks that defend against various cyber threats and vulnerabilities.

1.2.3 Penetration Tester (Red Team Member)

Responsibilities: Penetration testers, also known as ethical hackers, simulate cyberattacks to identify vulnerabilities in systems and applications. They conduct controlled testing, employing the same tactics as malicious actors to assess an organization's defenses. Following the engagement, penetration testers provide detailed reports on their findings and recommend remediation strategies.

Required Skills:

- Strong understanding of various attack vectors and exploitation techniques.
- Proficiency in penetration testing tools (e.g., Metasploit, Burp Suite, Nmap).
- Knowledge of programming and scripting languages.
- Familiarity with regulatory compliance and security standards.

Importance: Penetration testers are crucial for proactively identifying and addressing vulnerabilities, enabling organizations to strengthen their security posture.

1.2.4 Incident Responder

Responsibilities: Incident responders are responsible for managing and mitigating security incidents. They investigate breaches, analyze the impact of incidents, and implement response plans to contain and remediate threats. Incident responders also play a key role in post-incident analysis, helping organizations learn from security events.

Required Skills:

- Strong analytical and problem-solving abilities.
- Familiarity with incident response frameworks and methodologies (e.g., NIST, SANS).
- Proficiency in forensics tools and techniques.
- Excellent communication skills to collaborate with various stakeholders.

Importance: Incident responders are vital for minimizing the damage caused by security incidents and ensuring that organizations can recover swiftly and effectively.

1.2.5 Security Architect

Responsibilities: Security architects are responsible for designing and implementing an organization's security framework. They assess existing security measures, identify weaknesses, and develop comprehensive security strategies that align with business objectives. Security architects also evaluate new technologies and ensure they integrate seamlessly into the overall security architecture.

Required Skills:

- Extensive knowledge of security technologies and methodologies.
- Strong understanding of risk management principles.
- Experience in network and application architecture.
- Excellent communication and leadership skills.

Importance: Security architects provide the strategic direction for an organization's security initiatives, ensuring that security is embedded in all aspects of the organization's operations.

1.2.6 Chief Information Security Officer (CISO)

Responsibilities: The CISO is the executive responsible for an organization's information security strategy. This role involves overseeing the entire cybersecurity team, ensuring compliance with regulations, and communicating security risks to executive leadership and the board of directors. The CISO develops security policies and programs that protect the organization's assets and reputation.

Required Skills:

- Strong leadership and management skills.
- Extensive knowledge of cybersecurity principles and best practices.
- Excellent communication and presentation abilities.
- Experience in risk management and compliance frameworks.

Importance: The CISO plays a crucial role in shaping an organization's security culture and strategy, ensuring that cybersecurity is prioritized at all levels of the organization.

1.2.7 Compliance and Risk Management Specialist

Responsibilities: Compliance and risk management specialists focus on ensuring that organizations adhere to relevant regulations, standards, and policies. They assess risks to information assets, conduct audits, and develop compliance programs. Their work is essential for avoiding legal penalties and maintaining customer trust.

Required Skills:

- Strong understanding of regulatory frameworks (e.g., GDPR, HIPAA, PCI-DSS).
- Knowledge of risk assessment methodologies.
- Excellent analytical and problem-solving abilities.
- Strong communication skills for reporting findings and recommendations.

Importance: Compliance and risk management specialists help organizations navigate the complex landscape of regulations, ensuring that security measures align with legal and industry requirements.

1.2.8 Security Trainer and Awareness Specialist

Responsibilities: Security trainers and awareness specialists are responsible for educating employees about cybersecurity best practices and promoting a culture of security within the organization. They develop training programs, conduct workshops, and create awareness campaigns to inform employees about potential threats and how to recognize them.

Required Skills:

- Strong communication and presentation abilities.
- Knowledge of cybersecurity concepts and threats.
- Experience in developing educational materials and training programs.
- Ability to engage and motivate employees.

Importance: Security trainers and awareness specialists play a critical role in building a security-conscious workforce, reducing the likelihood of human error leading to security incidents.

Collaboration Among Cybersecurity Roles

While each cybersecurity role has distinct responsibilities, collaboration is essential for an effective security strategy. Cyber threats are dynamic and can evolve rapidly, making it necessary for teams to communicate and share information effectively. Here are a few ways in which collaboration enhances cybersecurity efforts:

Integrated Approach: By fostering collaboration among different roles, organizations can create a more integrated security approach. Security analysts, engineers, and incident responders can work together to identify and address vulnerabilities across the organization.

Knowledge Sharing: Regular communication among team members allows for the sharing of insights and experiences. Penetration testers can share findings with security engineers, leading to improved defenses. Similarly, incident responders can inform analysts about emerging threats and trends.

Cross-Training: Encouraging cross-training among team members can enhance overall team capabilities. For example, security analysts can learn about penetration testing techniques, while penetration testers can benefit from understanding incident response processes.

Enhanced Incident Response: During a security incident, a coordinated response from various roles is crucial. Incident responders, security analysts, and compliance specialists must work together to ensure a swift and effective response to mitigate damage.

Continuous Improvement: Collaborating allows organizations to learn from security incidents and red team engagements, leading to continuous improvement in security practices. By analyzing past events, teams can refine their strategies and bolster defenses.

The cybersecurity landscape is complex and constantly evolving, necessitating a diverse range of roles to effectively protect organizations from cyber threats. Each role, from security analysts to compliance specialists, contributes unique skills and perspectives to a comprehensive security strategy. By fostering collaboration and knowledge sharing among these roles, organizations can enhance their security posture and better prepare for the challenges posed by the digital world. As cyber threats continue to evolve, the importance of clearly defined roles and teamwork in cybersecurity will remain paramount, enabling organizations to respond effectively to a dynamic threat landscape.

1.3 Significance of Red Team Operations

Red team operations play an essential role in modern cybersecurity strategies, providing organizations with a proactive approach to identify and address vulnerabilities before malicious actors can exploit them. By simulating real-world attacks, red teams offer a unique perspective on security—one that mirrors the tactics, techniques, and procedures (TTPs) used by adversaries. This section explores the significance of red team operations in enhancing an organization's overall security posture, improving incident response, promoting a culture of continuous improvement, and meeting regulatory requirements.

1.3.1 Realistic Assessment of Security Posture

One of the most important benefits of red team operations is their ability to provide organizations with a realistic assessment of their security posture. Unlike traditional security assessments, such as vulnerability scanning or penetration testing, red teaming involves simulating advanced, multi-vector attacks that mimic the behavior of real-world adversaries. Red teamers think and act like cybercriminals, nation-state actors, or hacktivists, employing a variety of tactics—ranging from technical exploits to social engineering and physical security breaches—to uncover weaknesses.

This approach offers a deeper understanding of how well an organization's defenses can withstand a determined attacker. By identifying vulnerabilities that traditional assessments might miss, red team operations highlight not only technical gaps but also human and procedural weaknesses, providing a holistic view of security risks. These insights help organizations prioritize their security efforts and allocate resources to areas that are most vulnerable to attack.

1.3.2 Enhancing Incident Response Capabilities

Red team operations provide an invaluable opportunity to test an organization's incident response (IR) capabilities. During a red team engagement, the blue team (the organization's defensive security team) is often unaware that a simulation is taking place. This allows the red team to evaluate how effectively the blue team detects, responds to, and mitigates attacks in real time. Such exercises can expose weaknesses in incident response processes, such as delayed detection, inefficient communication, or ineffective remediation efforts.

The results of these exercises offer valuable feedback that can be used to improve the organization's IR protocols. By simulating sophisticated attacks, red teams challenge blue teams to think critically, refine their detection mechanisms, and streamline response actions. This leads to a more resilient and adaptive incident response strategy, ensuring that the organization is better prepared to handle actual attacks when they occur. Furthermore, red team exercises encourage collaboration between offensive (red) and defensive (blue) teams, fostering a culture of learning and continuous improvement.

1.3.3 Identifying Unknown Weaknesses

Traditional security assessments, such as vulnerability scanning and penetration testing, often focus on known vulnerabilities and predefined scopes. Red team operations, however, go beyond this approach by thinking outside the box and targeting areas that are not typically part of standard security testing. Red teamers may exploit weaknesses in physical security, social engineering opportunities, or flaws in organizational processes—areas that are often overlooked in routine security checks.

For instance, a red team may attempt to gain unauthorized physical access to a building, manipulate employees through phishing attacks, or exploit weaknesses in supply chain security. By uncovering these less obvious vulnerabilities, red team operations provide a more comprehensive picture of an organization's security risks. This proactive approach ensures that even hidden or unconventional attack vectors are addressed, greatly reducing the likelihood of a successful attack.

1.3.4 Stress Testing Organizational Resilience

Another key aspect of red team operations is their ability to stress test an organization's overall resilience to cyberattacks. Red team exercises often simulate extended and sophisticated attack campaigns, testing not only the effectiveness of technical defenses but also the organization's ability to maintain business continuity in the face of an attack.

By challenging an organization's infrastructure, employees, and processes, red teams can evaluate how well the organization can withstand pressure, adapt to evolving threats, and continue operating even when under attack. For example, a red team may test whether critical systems can remain functional during a simulated ransomware attack or assess how quickly key stakeholders can respond to a data breach. These stress tests reveal weaknesses in business continuity plans and disaster recovery strategies, enabling organizations to strengthen their resilience and prepare for worst-case scenarios.

1.3.5 Promoting a Culture of Continuous Improvement

Red team operations promote a mindset of continuous improvement within an organization. After each red team engagement, the findings and recommendations are used to refine security strategies, close identified gaps, and enhance overall defenses. This iterative process encourages organizations to constantly evaluate and improve their security posture, rather than relying on static or outdated measures.

Additionally, red team operations help create a culture of security awareness throughout the organization. By conducting realistic simulations, employees become more attuned to potential threats, such as phishing attacks or social engineering tactics. This heightened awareness leads to better adherence to security policies, stronger internal communication regarding security issues, and a more proactive approach to addressing vulnerabilities.

A culture of continuous improvement is essential in the rapidly evolving cybersecurity landscape, where attackers are constantly developing new techniques. Red team operations ensure that organizations stay ahead of emerging threats by regularly testing their defenses and making ongoing adjustments to their security strategies.

1.3.6 Meeting Regulatory and Compliance Requirements

In many industries, regulatory and compliance requirements mandate that organizations conduct regular security assessments and demonstrate their commitment to safeguarding sensitive data. Red team operations are increasingly being recognized as a valuable component of compliance programs, as they provide organizations with a thorough and realistic evaluation of their security defenses.

For example, frameworks such as the National Institute of Standards and Technology (NIST) and the Payment Card Industry Data Security Standard (PCI DSS) require organizations to assess their security posture and perform regular testing. Red team operations can fulfill these requirements by demonstrating that the organization is proactively identifying and mitigating risks through comprehensive security assessments.

Furthermore, the detailed reports generated after red team engagements serve as evidence of an organization's commitment to security, which can be presented during audits or reviews. By incorporating red team operations into their security and compliance programs, organizations not only meet regulatory obligations but also demonstrate a proactive approach to protecting their assets and customer data.

1.3.7 Adapting to Evolving Threat Landscapes

Cyber threats are constantly evolving, with attackers developing new techniques, tools, and tactics to breach defenses. Red team operations are particularly valuable because they enable organizations to test their security defenses against the latest and most sophisticated attack vectors. Red teams stay informed about emerging threats and continuously adapt their tactics to simulate the most current and realistic attack scenarios.

This adaptability is crucial for organizations that want to stay ahead of cybercriminals. By regularly conducting red team engagements, organizations can ensure that their security measures are effective against new and evolving threats. In contrast, relying solely on traditional security assessments may leave organizations vulnerable to novel attacks that have not yet been widely recognized.

Moreover, red team operations encourage organizations to think critically about future threats and develop long-term strategies for defending against them. This forward-thinking approach helps organizations build security infrastructures that are more resilient to both current and emerging risks.

Red team operations are a vital element of a comprehensive cybersecurity strategy. By simulating realistic attacks, red teams provide organizations with a detailed and holistic assessment of their security posture, identify unknown vulnerabilities, and test their incident response capabilities. Beyond addressing technical weaknesses, red team engagements stress-test organizational resilience, promote continuous improvement, and ensure compliance with regulatory requirements. Most importantly, they help organizations stay ahead of evolving threats, fostering a proactive and adaptive security culture. As cyber threats continue to grow in complexity, the significance of red team operations will only increase, making them an indispensable tool for organizations committed to robust cybersecurity defenses.

Chapter 2: Understanding the Threat Landscape

In this chapter, we delve into the intricate and ever-evolving landscape of cyber threats that organizations face today. Understanding this landscape is crucial for effective red teaming, as it provides the context in which vulnerabilities are exploited and attacks are carried out. We will explore current trends in cyber threats, identifying the motivations behind these attacks, and the tactics employed by adversaries. By examining common attack vectors, such as phishing, malware, and insider threats, readers will gain insights into how attackers operate and the methods they use to compromise systems. Additionally, this chapter will present notable case studies of major breaches, illustrating the real-world implications of inadequate security measures and highlighting the lessons learned. Armed with this knowledge, readers will be better equipped to anticipate potential threats and develop strategies to fortify their defenses in an increasingly hostile digital environment.

2.1 Current Trends in Cyber Threats

As the digital landscape continues to evolve, so do the tactics and techniques employed by cybercriminals. The modern threat landscape is marked by increasingly sophisticated attacks, rapid technological advancements, and a growing reliance on digital infrastructure, making it crucial for organizations to stay informed about current cyber threat trends. This section outlines key trends in cyber threats, offering insight into the types of attacks that pose the most significant risks today, the motivations behind them, and how organizations can prepare to defend against them.

2.1.1 Ransomware Evolution

Ransomware has emerged as one of the most pervasive and damaging cyber threats in recent years, evolving from simple attacks targeting individual users to highly sophisticated operations against large corporations, healthcare providers, and even critical infrastructure. Modern ransomware attacks have become more targeted and complex, with cybercriminals employing a variety of advanced techniques to maximize their impact and financial gain.

Double Extortion Tactics: One notable development in ransomware is the rise of double extortion tactics, in which attackers not only encrypt an organization's data but also exfiltrate sensitive information. This allows cybercriminals to threaten the victim with public exposure of the stolen data if the ransom is not paid, adding an additional layer of pressure to comply with their demands. This tactic has been particularly effective in industries such as healthcare and finance, where data confidentiality is critical.

Ransomware-as-a-Service (RaaS): Another trend driving the proliferation of ransomware is the growth of Ransomware-as-a-Service (RaaS) platforms. These platforms enable less technically skilled attackers to launch sophisticated ransomware campaigns by providing pre-built tools and infrastructure for a share of the profits. RaaS has lowered the barrier to entry for cybercriminals, contributing to the widespread nature of ransomware attacks.

Targeting Critical Infrastructure: Recent ransomware attacks have increasingly focused on critical infrastructure, such as energy providers, transportation systems, and healthcare organizations. The high stakes involved in these sectors, where downtime can have life-threatening consequences, often lead victims to pay ransoms quickly to restore operations. This trend has raised significant concerns about the potential for ransomware to disrupt essential services on a national or even global scale.

2.1.2 Supply Chain Attacks

Supply chain attacks have gained prominence as a particularly dangerous form of cyber threat, targeting the interconnected nature of modern businesses. Instead of attacking a company directly, cybercriminals compromise a third-party vendor or supplier with access to the target organization's network. This allows attackers to infiltrate multiple organizations simultaneously, often with devastating consequences.

Notable Incidents: High-profile supply chain attacks, such as the SolarWinds breach and the Kaseya ransomware attack, have underscored the potential scale and impact of these types of threats. In the SolarWinds attack, cybercriminals inserted malicious code into the company's software updates, which were then distributed to numerous government agencies and private sector organizations, leading to widespread data breaches.

Growing Complexity: The complexity of supply chain attacks makes them particularly challenging to defend against. Organizations often rely on a vast network of third-party vendors and partners, each with its own potential vulnerabilities. Cybercriminals exploit these relationships, using compromised suppliers as entry points into more secure environments.

Mitigating the Risk: To mitigate the risk of supply chain attacks, organizations must implement rigorous vendor management practices, including regular security assessments of third-party suppliers, monitoring for suspicious activity, and ensuring that partners adhere to strong cybersecurity standards.

2.1.3 Phishing and Social Engineering

Despite advances in cybersecurity technology, phishing and social engineering attacks remain among the most common and effective methods used by cybercriminals to gain unauthorized access to systems and data. These attacks exploit human behavior, relying on deception and manipulation to trick individuals into revealing sensitive information or performing actions that compromise security.

Spear Phishing: While traditional phishing campaigns often cast a wide net, modern spear phishing attacks are highly targeted, focusing on specific individuals or organizations. Attackers research their targets in-depth, crafting convincing emails or messages that appear legitimate. These messages may contain malicious links, attachments, or requests for sensitive information, such as login credentials or financial data.

Business Email Compromise (BEC): Business Email Compromise (BEC) is a specific type of phishing attack in which cybercriminals impersonate executives, vendors, or trusted partners to deceive employees into transferring money or sharing confidential information. BEC attacks have resulted in significant financial losses for organizations across various sectors, with attackers often using email spoofing or compromised accounts to increase the authenticity of their communications.

Voice Phishing (Vishing) and Smishing: In addition to email-based phishing attacks, cybercriminals are increasingly using other communication channels, such as phone calls (vishing) and text messages (smishing), to target individuals. These attacks often involve impersonating trusted entities, such as banks or government agencies, and can be highly convincing, leading victims to disclose sensitive information or make fraudulent payments.

2.1.4 Advanced Persistent Threats (APTs)

Advanced Persistent Threats (APTs) refer to highly sophisticated and prolonged cyberattacks, often carried out by nation-state actors or organized cybercriminal groups. APTs typically target large organizations, government agencies, or critical infrastructure, with the goal of gaining long-term access to sensitive data or disrupting operations.

Stealth and Persistence: APT attacks are characterized by their stealth and persistence, with attackers often remaining undetected within a network for extended periods. Once inside, they move laterally through the network, collecting valuable information or compromising critical systems. APTs frequently use custom malware and zero-day vulnerabilities, making them difficult to detect and mitigate using traditional security tools.

Nation-State Involvement: Many APT groups are backed by nation-states and are often motivated by political, economic, or military goals. These attacks can have far-reaching implications, including espionage, intellectual property theft, and disruption of critical infrastructure. Recent examples include attacks attributed to groups such as APT29 (linked to Russia) and APT41 (linked to China).

Defensive Measures: Defending against APTs requires a multi-layered security strategy, including advanced threat detection technologies, network segmentation, continuous monitoring, and incident response planning. Organizations must be prepared to detect and respond to suspicious activity quickly to minimize the damage caused by these long-term attacks.

2.1.5 Zero-Day Exploits

Zero-day exploits refer to attacks that take advantage of vulnerabilities in software or hardware that are unknown to the vendor and, therefore, have no available patches. These exploits are highly valuable to cybercriminals and nation-state actors because they allow attackers to bypass security defenses before the vulnerability is publicly disclosed and fixed.

Rising Use in Targeted Attacks: Zero-day exploits have become a common tool in targeted attacks, particularly those carried out by APT groups and cybercriminals seeking high-value targets. These exploits often target widely used software, such as operating systems, web browsers, or enterprise applications, making them particularly dangerous.

Challenges in Detection and Mitigation: Because zero-day exploits target unknown vulnerabilities, traditional security tools may be ineffective in detecting and preventing them. Organizations must rely on advanced security measures, such as behavior-based detection and threat intelligence, to identify and respond to these threats. Keeping software up to date and implementing strong patch management practices are also critical in reducing the risk of zero-day attacks.

2.1.6 Insider Threats

While much attention is focused on external cyber threats, insider threats—security risks that originate from within an organization—continue to be a significant concern. Insider threats can involve employees, contractors, or other trusted individuals who intentionally or unintentionally compromise an organization's security.

Types of Insider Threats: Insider threats can take many forms, including:

- Malicious insiders who deliberately steal data, sabotage systems, or engage in fraud for personal gain or to harm the organization.
- Negligent insiders who unintentionally cause security breaches through poor security practices, such as using weak passwords or falling victim to phishing attacks.
- Compromised insiders who are coerced or blackmailed into assisting external attackers, often under duress.

Mitigating Insider Threats: To reduce the risk of insider threats, organizations should implement strict access controls, monitor user activity, and foster a culture of security awareness. Conducting background checks, offering regular cybersecurity training, and using behavioral analytics to detect unusual activity can also help mitigate insider threats.

The current trends in cyber threats underscore the need for organizations to stay vigilant and adapt to an ever-changing threat landscape. As cybercriminals become more sophisticated and new attack vectors emerge, businesses must implement a multi-faceted security strategy that includes advanced threat detection, employee education, and continuous monitoring. By staying informed about these evolving threats and taking proactive measures, organizations can better protect their assets, data, and reputation from increasingly complex cyberattacks.

2.2 Common Attack Vectors

In the modern cybersecurity landscape, attackers utilize a variety of methods, known as attack vectors, to gain unauthorized access to systems, disrupt operations, or steal sensitive information. Understanding these common attack vectors is critical for defending against cyber threats and implementing effective security measures. This section explores the most prevalent attack vectors, shedding light on how cybercriminals exploit vulnerabilities in networks, applications, and human behavior.

2.2.1 Phishing and Social Engineering

Phishing and social engineering attacks are among the most common and effective attack vectors, leveraging human vulnerabilities rather than technical flaws. These attacks manipulate individuals into revealing sensitive information, such as login credentials or financial data, or performing actions that compromise security.

Email Phishing: One of the most widespread forms of social engineering, phishing often involves sending fraudulent emails that appear to come from legitimate sources, such as banks, colleagues, or trusted organizations. These emails may contain malicious links, attachments, or requests for sensitive information. Attackers often use techniques like spoofing to make the emails appear more credible.

Spear Phishing: Unlike traditional phishing campaigns that target large numbers of users, spear phishing is highly targeted. Attackers carefully research their victims and craft personalized messages designed to trick them into divulging confidential information. These messages often appear to come from trusted sources within the organization, such as a manager or IT department, increasing the likelihood of success.

Pretexting and Baiting: Pretexting involves creating a fabricated scenario to convince the victim to share information or perform an action, often by impersonating a trusted authority figure. Baiting, on the other hand, lures victims into providing information by offering something desirable, such as a free download or prize, that is actually malware-laden.

Vishing and Smishing: Cybercriminals are expanding beyond email, using phone calls (vishing) and text messages (smishing) to carry out social engineering attacks. In these cases, attackers impersonate banks, government agencies, or other trusted entities to manipulate victims into revealing sensitive information.

2.2.2 Malware and Malicious Software

Malware, short for malicious software, is a broad category of attack vectors that includes viruses, worms, Trojans, ransomware, spyware, and more. Malware is designed to infiltrate systems, steal data, or cause damage, often without the user's knowledge.

Viruses and Worms: These are two of the earliest forms of malware. A virus attaches itself to legitimate programs or files and spreads when those programs are executed. It can corrupt data, disrupt operations, or allow attackers to control a compromised system. A worm, unlike a virus, can spread without user interaction, often replicating across networks to infect multiple systems.

Trojans: Trojans disguise themselves as legitimate software but contain malicious code that allows attackers to gain control of a system or steal information. Once installed, Trojans can create backdoors, giving attackers persistent access to the system and enabling further attacks like data exfiltration or ransomware installation.

Ransomware: Ransomware encrypts an organization's data and demands payment, often in cryptocurrency, in exchange for the decryption key. Recent ransomware trends involve double extortion tactics, where attackers also steal sensitive data and threaten to release it publicly if the ransom is not paid. Ransomware has become a major threat to businesses and critical infrastructure, as it can cause significant financial losses and operational downtime.

Spyware and Keyloggers: Spyware is designed to secretly monitor user activity, collecting sensitive information such as browsing history, login credentials, or financial data. Keyloggers, a subset of spyware, record keystrokes to capture passwords and other confidential information. These types of malware are often used in targeted attacks to gather intelligence for further exploitation.

2.2.3 Network Attacks

Attackers frequently target network vulnerabilities to gain unauthorized access, intercept data, or disrupt communication. Network-based attack vectors are often aimed at exploiting weaknesses in network protocols, poorly configured systems, or unsecured network devices.

Man-in-the-Middle (MitM) Attacks: In a MitM attack, the attacker intercepts communication between two parties, allowing them to eavesdrop on, alter, or inject malicious content into the conversation. This type of attack can be carried out on nsecure public Wi-Fi networks, where attackers intercept traffic between the user and the network.

Denial-of-Service (DoS) and Distributed Denial-of-Service (DDoS): DoS and DDoS attacks aim to overwhelm a target's network, server, or application with excessive traffic, causing it to crash or become unavailable. While a DoS attack originates from a single source, a DDoS attack involves multiple compromised systems (often part of a botnet) flooding the target. These attacks can cripple online services and disrupt business operations.

DNS Spoofing and Poisoning: DNS spoofing, also known as DNS poisoning, involves corrupting the Domain Name System (DNS) to redirect traffic from legitimate websites to malicious ones. This can lead to phishing sites, malware downloads, or compromised login credentials. Attackers use DNS spoofing to deceive users into interacting with malicious content without their knowledge.

Packet Sniffing: Packet sniffing tools allow attackers to capture and analyze network traffic, potentially exposing sensitive data like passwords, emails, and other unencrypted information. These tools are often used in conjunction with MitM attacks, allowing attackers to gain insight into network communications and exploit vulnerabilities.

2.2.4 Application and Software Exploits

Exploiting vulnerabilities in applications and software is a common attack vector, often targeting outdated or misconfigured systems. These exploits can lead to unauthorized access, privilege escalation, or data theft.

SQL Injection: SQL injection attacks target web applications by inserting malicious SQL queries into input fields, such as login forms or search bars. If the application does not properly sanitize user input, the attacker can execute arbitrary SQL commands, allowing them to retrieve, modify, or delete data from the application's database.

Cross-Site Scripting (XSS): XSS attacks occur when an attacker injects malicious scripts into web pages viewed by other users. These scripts can steal session cookies, redirect users to malicious sites, or manipulate web content. There are two primary types of XSS: Stored XSS, where the malicious code is permanently stored on the server, and Reflected XSS, where the malicious code is delivered via a URL or user input.

Remote Code Execution (RCE): RCE vulnerabilities allow attackers to execute arbitrary code on a target system remotely. This can lead to full system compromise, giving attackers control over the affected system. RCE vulnerabilities are often found in poorly secured or outdated software, making timely patching critical to prevent exploitation.

Zero-Day Exploits: Zero-day exploits take advantage of vulnerabilities that have not yet been discovered or patched by software vendors. These are especially dangerous because they can bypass existing security measures, leaving organizations vulnerable until a patch is available. Zero-day exploits are frequently used in targeted attacks by advanced persistent threat (APT) groups and are highly valuable on the black market.

2.2.5 Credential-Based Attacks

Credential-based attacks focus on stealing or guessing login credentials, such as usernames and passwords, to gain unauthorized access to systems and accounts. These attacks often target weak or reused passwords, making strong password hygiene a critical defense measure.

Brute Force Attacks: In brute force attacks, attackers use automated tools to systematically guess passwords by trying every possible combination. While brute force attacks can be time-consuming, weak or commonly used passwords can be cracked quickly. Tools like dictionary attacks, which use lists of common passwords, can expedite the process.

Credential Stuffing: Credential stuffing occurs when attackers use stolen usernames and passwords from one data breach to attempt logins on other platforms. Since many users reuse passwords across multiple accounts, credential stuffing is an effective way for attackers to gain access to multiple systems with minimal effort.

Password Spraying: In contrast to brute force attacks, which target a single account, password spraying involves trying a small number of commonly used passwords across many accounts. This technique is designed to evade detection by limiting the number of failed login attempts per account, reducing the chances of triggering account lockouts.

2.2.6 Physical Security Breaches

While much of cybersecurity focuses on digital threats, physical security breaches remain a common attack vector. Attackers may exploit weak physical security controls to gain unauthorized access to sensitive areas, devices, or data.

Tailgating and Piggybacking: Tailgating occurs when an unauthorized person follows an authorized individual into a secure area, bypassing physical access controls like keycards or biometric scanners. Piggybacking is a similar technique but often involves the authorized individual knowingly allowing the attacker to enter.

Device Theft: Theft of laptops, smartphones, and other devices can lead to unauthorized access to sensitive data. While encryption and strong access controls can mitigate the risk, attackers may still attempt to extract data from stolen devices or use them as entry points into the organization's network.

Keylogging Devices: Physical keylogging devices can be installed on a victim's keyboard or computer to capture keystrokes, revealing sensitive information such as passwords and confidential data. These devices can be discreetly installed in high-traffic areas, such as public workstations or employee desks.

Understanding common attack vectors is fundamental to developing an effective cybersecurity defense strategy. Cybercriminals exploit a wide range of vulnerabilities, from social engineering tactics and malware to network and application exploits. By recognizing these attack vectors and implementing multi-layered defenses, organizations can significantly reduce their exposure to cyber threats and better protect their systems, data, and users from compromise.

2.3 Case Studies of Major Breaches

Major data breaches serve as crucial learning experiences, offering valuable insights into the tactics, techniques, and procedures (TTPs) employed by attackers and the vulnerabilities exploited during these incidents. By examining case studies of prominent cyberattacks, organizations can better understand the complexities of modern cyber threats and implement stronger defenses. This section highlights key examples of major breaches, focusing on the methods used, the impact of the attacks, and the lessons learned from each case.

2.3.1 Target Breach (2013)

The 2013 Target data breach is one of the most well-known cyberattacks in retail history, affecting approximately 110 million customers and exposing sensitive information such as credit card numbers, personal contact information, and other personal details. The breach underscored the importance of vendor security and revealed how attackers can exploit weak links in the supply chain.

Attack Vector: The attackers gained access to Target's network through a third-party HVAC vendor. The vendor's credentials were compromised via a phishing email, granting the attackers access to Target's network. Once inside, the attackers used this foothold to install malware on Target's point-of-sale (POS) systems, allowing them to collect payment card data as customers made purchases in-store.

Impact: The breach compromised 40 million credit and debit card numbers, along with 70 million customer records containing personal details such as names, addresses, and phone numbers. Target faced significant financial repercussions, including settlements with banks and credit card companies, as well as a tarnished reputation and loss of consumer trust.

Lessons Learned:

- **Vendor Security**: The breach highlighted the importance of securing third-party vendor access to critical systems. Implementing stricter vendor management practices, including conducting security assessments and limiting vendor access based on the principle of least privilege, could have mitigated the attack.
- **Network Segmentation**: Proper network segmentation could have prevented the attackers from moving laterally across Target's network and accessing the POS systems.
- **Real-Time Monitoring**: Enhanced real-time monitoring and threat detection might have allowed Target to identify the breach earlier, minimizing the damage.

2.3.2 Equifax Breach (2017)

The Equifax breach of 2017, one of the largest data breaches in history, exposed the sensitive personal information of over 147 million individuals, including Social Security numbers, birth dates, addresses, and in some cases, driver's license numbers. This breach had long-lasting effects on victims, given the highly sensitive nature of the data.

Attack Vector: The attackers exploited a known vulnerability in Apache Struts, a widely used web application framework. The vulnerability (CVE-2017-5638) had been disclosed months earlier, but Equifax had failed to apply the necessary patch in a timely manner. Once inside the network, the attackers were able to exfiltrate data over several weeks before the breach was discovered.

Impact: The breach resulted in massive financial losses for Equifax, including regulatory fines, legal settlements, and the cost of credit monitoring services for affected individuals. Additionally, the breach severely damaged Equifax's reputation as a major credit reporting agency.

Lessons Learned:

- **Patch Management**: The Equifax breach underscored the critical importance of timely patch management. Regularly updating software and applying patches as soon as they are released can significantly reduce the risk of exploitation.
- **Data Encryption**: Sensitive data, such as Social Security numbers, should be encrypted both in transit and at rest to protect it from theft. Equifax's failure to properly encrypt sensitive data contributed to the scale of the breach.
- **Incident Response**: Equifax's delayed response to the breach exacerbated its impact. Having a well-developed incident response plan and conducting regular security audits could have mitigated the extent of the data exposure.

2.3.3 Yahoo Breach (2013-2014)

The Yahoo breaches of 2013 and 2014 collectively exposed the personal data of 3 billion users, making it the largest data breach in history. The stolen data included names, email addresses, phone numbers, birthdates, hashed passwords, and, in some cases, security questions and answers. The breach was attributed to state-sponsored attackers, raising concerns about nation-state involvement in cybercrime.

Attack Vector: The attackers used spear phishing techniques to target Yahoo employees, eventually gaining access to the company's user database. Once inside the network, the attackers were able to extract vast amounts of user data over an extended period without being detected.

Impact: Yahoo's handling of the breach, particularly its delayed disclosure of the incidents, led to a loss of trust among users and severely impacted the company's value. Yahoo's acquisition by Verizon was negatively affected, with the company losing hundreds of millions of dollars in valuation.

Lessons Learned:

- **Employee Training**: The breach emphasized the importance of employee cybersecurity awareness and training, especially regarding spear phishing and social engineering attacks. Yahoo could have prevented the initial compromise by educating employees about recognizing phishing attempts.
- **Comprehensive Security Measures**: The breach highlighted the need for stronger encryption practices, particularly for sensitive information like security questions and answers, which were not properly protected in Yahoo's systems.
- **Timely Disclosure**: Yahoo's delayed disclosure of the breach resulted in regulatory scrutiny and damaged its reputation. Organizations should have clear

policies for timely breach disclosure to minimize the fallout and maintain customer trust.

2.3.4 Marriott International Breach (2014-2018)

The Marriott International breach, discovered in 2018, affected approximately 500 million guests, with sensitive information such as passport numbers, credit card details, and reservation histories being exposed. The breach had persisted since 2014, when attackers compromised Starwood Hotels' systems, which Marriott acquired in 2016.

Attack Vector: The breach stemmed from the compromise of Starwood Hotels' reservation system. Attackers had access to the system for four years, during which they exfiltrated guest information. The attackers used malware and other advanced persistent threat (APT) tactics to maintain their presence undetected for an extended period.

Impact: The breach resulted in severe reputational damage for Marriott and significant financial losses, including regulatory fines and legal settlements. The exposure of passport numbers raised concerns about identity theft and the long-term impact on affected individuals.

Lessons Learned:

- **Due Diligence in Mergers and Acquisitions**: The Marriott breach demonstrated the need for thorough cybersecurity due diligence during mergers and acquisitions. Marriott failed to identify the vulnerability in Starwood's systems during the acquisition process, which allowed the attackers to continue their operations undetected.
- **Data Protection**: The breach underscored the importance of encrypting sensitive data, such as passport numbers and credit card details. Improved data protection measures could have reduced the scope of the breach.
- **Extended Threat Detection**: The length of time attackers remained undetected highlighted the need for continuous monitoring and advanced threat detection systems. Organizations should deploy tools capable of identifying anomalies and potential threats over extended periods.

2.3.5 Colonial Pipeline Ransomware Attack (2021)

The Colonial Pipeline ransomware attack in May 2021 disrupted the largest fuel pipeline in the United States, causing widespread panic and fuel shortages along the East

Coast. The attack was carried out by the cybercriminal group DarkSide, which used ransomware to encrypt Colonial Pipeline's IT systems, forcing the company to shut down its operations.

Attack Vector: The attackers used compromised credentials to gain access to Colonial Pipeline's network. Once inside, they deployed ransomware that encrypted the company's files, rendering critical systems inoperable. The company chose to shut down its operations to prevent the ransomware from spreading to its operational technology (OT) network.

Impact: The attack caused widespread fuel shortages, leading to panic buying and price spikes in multiple states. Colonial Pipeline paid a ransom of $4.4 million in Bitcoin to regain access to its systems, though law enforcement later recovered a portion of the ransom.

Lessons Learned:

- **Segmentation of IT and OT Systems**: The attack demonstrated the importance of segmenting IT and OT networks to prevent malware from spreading across critical systems. Isolating operational technology from the broader corporate network could have mitigated the impact of the ransomware attack.
- **Zero Trust Architecture**: Adopting a zero-trust security model, where access is strictly limited and continuously verified, could have prevented attackers from moving laterally within the network after compromising credentials.
- **Incident Response and Backup Strategies**: The attack underscored the need for robust incident response plans and regular backup strategies. Colonial Pipeline's reliance on paying the ransom highlighted the importance of having secure, offline backups to recover from ransomware without engaging with the attackers.

These case studies of major breaches reveal several common themes, including the exploitation of unpatched vulnerabilities, phishing attacks, poor vendor security, and a lack of timely detection and response. By analyzing these incidents, organizations can better understand the tactics used by attackers and take proactive steps to improve their security posture, such as enforcing strong patch management, implementing multi-factor authentication, encrypting sensitive data, and maintaining a robust incident response plan.

Chapter 3: Building a Red Team

In this chapter, we focus on the essential components and considerations for establishing a successful red team within an organization. Building a red team involves more than just assembling skilled individuals; it requires a strategic approach to developing a cohesive unit capable of simulating real-world attacks effectively. We will begin by discussing the diverse skill sets and expertise necessary for red team members, emphasizing both technical proficiencies and soft skills that foster collaboration and creativity. Next, we will outline the various roles within a red team, including penetration testers, threat hunters, and social engineers, highlighting their unique contributions to the team's objectives. Finally, we will explore the importance of ongoing training and development, emphasizing the need for continuous learning and adaptation to stay ahead of emerging threats. By the end of this chapter, readers will have a comprehensive understanding of how to build a robust red team that can enhance their organization's overall security posture and proactively identify vulnerabilities.

3.1 Skills and Expertise Needed

Building an effective red team requires a diverse set of skills and expertise, as red team operations encompass a wide range of tasks, from reconnaissance to exploitation and reporting. These professionals need to possess both deep technical knowledge and the ability to think creatively, simulating the tactics and mindset of malicious actors. This section outlines the key skills and areas of expertise essential for successful red team operations.

3.1.1 Offensive Security Skills

At the core of red teaming is the ability to conduct offensive security operations, including penetration testing and vulnerability exploitation. Red team members must be skilled in simulating real-world attacks to test and assess the security posture of an organization.

Penetration Testing: Red teamers need to have extensive experience with penetration testing tools and techniques. This includes knowledge of network penetration, web application security testing, wireless security testing, and testing against APIs. Being proficient with tools like Metasploit, Burp Suite, Nmap, and custom scripts is essential for identifying vulnerabilities and weaknesses.

Exploitation Techniques: Beyond finding vulnerabilities, red teamers must have the skills to exploit them. This includes understanding common exploitation frameworks and techniques for privilege escalation, lateral movement, and persistence. Familiarity with zero-day exploits, social engineering strategies, and phishing attacks also plays a significant role in mimicking real-world adversaries.

Network and Application Security: A solid understanding of network protocols, operating systems, and security architectures is essential. Red teamers should know how to exploit vulnerabilities in networking devices, web applications, databases, and cloud environments. This includes knowing how to navigate firewall rules, detect misconfigurations, and exploit poor security practices in both internal and external-facing applications.

3.1.2 Reconnaissance and Information Gathering

Reconnaissance, or the process of gathering intelligence on a target, is a critical phase of red team operations. Successful red teamers excel in gathering valuable information while remaining undetected by security defenses.

Open Source Intelligence (OSINT): OSINT involves using publicly available information to gather intelligence on the target organization and its employees. This includes searching for exposed data on social media platforms, job boards, company websites, and other public-facing services. Red teamers should be adept at identifying sensitive information, such as email addresses, software versions, and organizational structures, which can be used for further attacks.

Network Scanning and Enumeration: Red teamers must be proficient in identifying live hosts, open ports, services, and network topology. Tools like Nmap, Netcat, and mass scanning utilities are commonly used for network reconnaissance. Red teamers need to understand how to map out internal networks and identify critical infrastructure components, such as databases, application servers, and network appliances, to plan their attack paths.

Human Reconnaissance: Social engineering is often a key component of red teaming. Red teamers need to understand human behavior and the psychology of manipulation. This includes conducting pretexting, phishing, and physical surveillance. Being able to effectively gather information about employees and use it to launch targeted attacks is crucial.

3.1.3 Programming and Scripting

While many security tools are available, the ability to write custom scripts and code gives red teamers an edge in crafting unique attacks and bypassing security measures. Scripting and programming skills enable red teamers to automate tasks, customize exploits, and develop new tools tailored to specific environments.

Scripting Languages: Proficiency in scripting languages like Python, Bash, and PowerShell is essential. Red teamers often use these languages to automate reconnaissance tasks, develop custom payloads, or manipulate files and processes during an engagement. For example, Python is frequently used to create exploits and automate the scanning of large networks.

Exploit Development: Red teamers with advanced programming skills can develop or modify existing exploits to bypass security protections. Knowledge of low-level programming languages, such as C, C++, and assembly, is crucial for those involved in exploit development or reverse engineering. These skills are particularly useful for developing zero-day exploits or working in environments where off-the-shelf tools are insufficient.

Web Application and API Exploitation: As web applications and APIs are increasingly common attack surfaces, red teamers need to understand web development languages like JavaScript, PHP, and HTML. This allows them to identify and exploit weaknesses like cross-site scripting (XSS), SQL injection, and API misconfigurations. Additionally, red teamers should understand web frameworks and how they interact with databases and cloud environments.

3.1.4 Adversary Simulation and Attack Scenarios

Red teaming goes beyond typical penetration testing by focusing on realistic adversary simulation. This involves emulating specific threat actors or attack scenarios to test an organization's defenses against particular types of threats.

Threat Modeling: Red teamers must be able to conduct threat modeling, which involves identifying and prioritizing potential threats based on an organization's assets, vulnerabilities, and likely adversaries. This requires an understanding of the threat landscape, including emerging attack techniques and the motivations of different types of adversaries, from nation-states to criminal groups.

Advanced Persistent Threat (APT) Simulation: Many red team exercises simulate APTs, which are stealthy, prolonged attacks carried out by well-funded adversaries. Red teamers need to be familiar with the TTPs used by APTs, such as custom malware, persistence techniques, and lateral movement strategies. Understanding how to evade detection by security tools (e.g., antivirus, intrusion detection systems, and endpoint detection and response tools) is a key part of this skill set.

Physical Security Assessments: In some cases, red teamers conduct physical security assessments by attempting to gain unauthorized access to buildings, server rooms, or other secure areas. Knowledge of physical bypass techniques, such as lock-picking, tailgating, and evading surveillance, is valuable for simulating insider threats or physical breach attempts.

3.1.5 Communication and Reporting Skills

While technical skills are paramount, red teamers must also be effective communicators, capable of conveying complex security issues to non-technical stakeholders. After an engagement, red teamers are responsible for presenting their findings and working with the organization's blue team to develop remediation strategies.

Report Writing: Red teamers need to produce comprehensive reports detailing the vulnerabilities they discovered, how they exploited them, and the potential impact on the organization. These reports must include clear, actionable recommendations for improving security. Strong report writing skills help ensure that the findings are understood and acted upon by senior management and technical teams alike.

Debriefing and Presentations: In addition to written reports, red teamers often present their findings in debriefing sessions with executives and technical staff. The ability to clearly explain complex attacks, communicate the severity of risks, and suggest mitigation strategies is essential for ensuring that the red team engagement leads to meaningful improvements.

Collaboration with Blue Teams: Red teamers should be able to work effectively with blue teams (defensive security teams) during post-engagement discussions. This requires the ability to share insights, identify areas of improvement, and help the blue team strengthen defenses against future attacks. Red teamers should also foster a collaborative relationship with other security professionals, facilitating knowledge sharing and continuous improvement.

The skills and expertise required for red team operations are multifaceted, blending technical prowess with creative problem-solving and strong communication abilities. From offensive security techniques to programming and adversary simulation, red teamers must be highly adaptable and resourceful in emulating real-world attacks. Additionally, the ability to effectively communicate findings and collaborate with defensive teams is critical to the success of red team engagements. By cultivating a diverse skill set, red team professionals can help organizations identify and address vulnerabilities before malicious actors exploit them.

3.2 Team Roles and Responsibilities

A successful red team is composed of professionals with specialized skills, each playing a critical role in the execution of simulated attacks and vulnerability assessments. Red team operations require collaboration, with each team member contributing to different stages of the engagement, from reconnaissance to post-exploitation and reporting. This section outlines the key roles within a red team and their specific responsibilities.

3.2.1 Red Team Leader

The Red Team Leader is responsible for overseeing the entire red team operation, ensuring that all objectives are met and that the team adheres to the scope and rules of engagement. This role requires both leadership and technical expertise, as the Red Team Leader must guide the team through complex attack scenarios while managing communication with stakeholders.

Responsibilities:

- **Planning and Scoping**: The Red Team Leader works closely with the client or internal stakeholders to define the scope, goals, and limitations of the engagement. This includes identifying key assets to be targeted, ensuring the rules of engagement are clear, and developing a timeline for the operation.
- **Strategy Development**: The leader devises the overall attack strategy, considering factors such as threat modeling, organizational weaknesses, and specific attack vectors that will be used. They ensure the strategy aligns with the objectives of the engagement and simulates realistic threats.
- **Coordination and Oversight**: Throughout the engagement, the Red Team Leader monitors progress, provides guidance, and resolves any issues that arise. They are responsible for ensuring that team members work efficiently and remain within the agreed-upon scope.

- **Communication and Reporting**: The Red Team Leader acts as the primary point of contact between the red team and the organization's senior management or blue team. They ensure that the findings are clearly communicated in both written reports and debriefing sessions, offering recommendations for remediation.

3.2.2 Reconnaissance Specialist

The Reconnaissance Specialist is tasked with gathering intelligence on the target organization during the initial phase of the red team engagement. This role requires expertise in information gathering, open-source intelligence (OSINT), and the ability to identify potential weaknesses before an attack is launched.

Responsibilities:

- **Information Gathering**: The Reconnaissance Specialist conducts OSINT activities, collecting data from public sources such as websites, social media, and employee profiles. They look for information that could be leveraged in an attack, such as exposed credentials, software versions, or network details.
- **Network Mapping**: This role involves scanning and mapping the target organization's network to identify live hosts, open ports, services, and potential vulnerabilities. Tools such as Nmap, Shodan, and mass scanning utilities are commonly used for this purpose.
- **Human Intelligence (HUMINT):** The Reconnaissance Specialist may also gather intelligence on key individuals within the organization, identifying potential targets for social engineering attacks. This includes analyzing employee behavior, social media activity, and job-related information that could help in crafting phishing campaigns or other social engineering attacks.
- **Pre-Attack Preparation**: The intelligence gathered by the Reconnaissance Specialist helps inform the rest of the red team, allowing them to develop targeted attack strategies. The specialist ensures that all necessary information is collected without triggering security defenses or alerting the organization to their presence.

3.2.3 Exploitation Specialist

The Exploitation Specialist is responsible for identifying vulnerabilities within the target's infrastructure and developing or utilizing exploits to gain unauthorized access. This role requires deep technical knowledge of security vulnerabilities, exploitation techniques, and offensive security tools.

Responsibilities:

- **Vulnerability Identification**: The Exploitation Specialist uses a variety of tools and manual techniques to identify security flaws within the organization's systems, networks, and applications. This includes web application vulnerabilities, misconfigured services, outdated software, and weak authentication mechanisms.
- **Developing Exploits**: In some cases, the specialist may need to develop custom exploits to target specific vulnerabilities that cannot be exploited with off-the-shelf tools. This involves writing code, reverse-engineering software, and understanding low-level system behaviors to craft effective exploits.
- **Exploitation and Privilege Escalation**: Once a vulnerability is identified, the Exploitation Specialist works to gain unauthorized access, escalate privileges, and maintain persistence within the compromised system. This may involve techniques such as local privilege escalation, lateral movement, and exploiting zero-day vulnerabilities.
- **Stealth and Evasion**: The Exploitation Specialist ensures that their actions remain undetected by the organization's security tools, such as intrusion detection systems (IDS), firewalls, and endpoint protection systems. This requires knowledge of evasion techniques, such as encrypting payloads, using stealthy malware, or blending in with legitimate traffic.

3.2.4 Social Engineering Specialist

The Social Engineering Specialist focuses on exploiting human vulnerabilities rather than technical ones. They use psychological manipulation to trick employees or insiders into divulging sensitive information or granting unauthorized access to systems and physical locations.

Responsibilities:

- **Phishing Campaigns**: The Social Engineering Specialist is often responsible for crafting and executing phishing attacks, which involve sending fraudulent emails that trick recipients into revealing login credentials or clicking malicious links. These campaigns can target individuals or entire departments.
- **Pretexting and Impersonation**: This specialist creates believable pretexts to engage with employees and extract information, often posing as a trusted figure such as an IT support technician or an external vendor. They may also impersonate key individuals within the organization to gain trust.

- **Physical Social Engineering**: In some cases, the specialist attempts to gain physical access to secure areas, such as data centers or server rooms, by manipulating security guards or employees. Techniques like tailgating (following someone through a secure door) or using fake credentials are commonly employed.
- **Exploiting Insider Information**: The Social Engineering Specialist uses information obtained from reconnaissance, such as personal details about employees, to craft more convincing attacks. They may also try to compromise employees through spear-phishing or other targeted social engineering techniques.

3.2.5 Red Team Developer

The Red Team Developer focuses on creating custom tools, scripts, and payloads for the engagement. This role is critical for bypassing security measures that off-the-shelf tools might not be able to overcome. The developer ensures that the red team has access to advanced, tailored attack vectors.

Responsibilities:

- **Custom Tool Development**: The Red Team Developer writes custom code and scripts for various phases of the engagement, including reconnaissance, exploitation, and post-exploitation. These tools may be used to automate tasks, exploit unique vulnerabilities, or bypass security controls.
- **Payload Design**: This specialist develops malware, rootkits, or other malicious payloads designed to infiltrate the target's systems while avoiding detection. They may modify existing exploits or develop entirely new ones based on the environment being tested.
- **Automation of Attacks**: The developer creates automation scripts to handle large-scale scanning, exploitation, and data exfiltration. By automating certain processes, they increase the efficiency and effectiveness of the red team during engagements.
- **Code Review and Testing**: To ensure that the tools and payloads function as intended, the developer conducts thorough testing and debugging. They also review existing code to identify potential weaknesses or improvements that can enhance the team's attack capabilities.

3.2.6 Post-Exploitation Specialist

The Post-Exploitation Specialist focuses on maintaining access, gathering valuable data, and ensuring that any actions taken during the engagement remain stealthy. This phase occurs after the initial exploitation and is crucial for assessing the depth of an organization's vulnerabilities.

Responsibilities:

- **Persistence and Lateral Movement**: The Post-Exploitation Specialist works to maintain access to compromised systems by establishing persistence mechanisms, such as installing backdoors or leveraging legitimate administrative tools. They also focus on moving laterally through the network, escalating privileges, and compromising additional systems.
- **Data Exfiltration**: This specialist identifies sensitive information such as intellectual property, personal data, or financial records and extracts it from the organization's systems. They ensure that the exfiltration process is stealthy, avoiding detection by security monitoring tools.
- **System Monitoring and Manipulation**: The Post-Exploitation Specialist monitors compromised systems to gather additional intelligence. They may manipulate system logs, hide traces of their activities, or collect information about network traffic, user behavior, or internal processes to further their objectives.
- **Privilege Escalation**: In cases where initial access is limited, the Post-Exploitation Specialist focuses on escalating privileges to gain full control over critical systems or domains, maximizing the damage potential of the attack.

Red team operations require a wide range of expertise, with each role contributing to different phases of an engagement. From leadership and coordination to exploitation and social engineering, the division of responsibilities allows the red team to simulate real-world attacks comprehensively. Each team member plays a critical role in identifying, exploiting, and assessing vulnerabilities, ensuring that the organization receives valuable insights into its security posture.

3.3 Training and Development

Continuous training and development are critical for red team members to stay at the cutting edge of offensive security. With the evolving landscape of cyber threats, red team professionals must regularly update their skills and knowledge to remain effective in simulating realistic adversarial behavior. This section discusses the importance of training, common methods of professional development, and strategies for red teams to maintain a high level of expertise.

3.3.1 Importance of Continuous Learning

Cybersecurity is a dynamic field, with new threats, vulnerabilities, and attack techniques emerging constantly. Red team professionals must stay ahead of these developments to accurately simulate real-world attacks and test an organization's defenses. Continuous learning helps red team members:

- **Keep up with emerging threats**: Attackers regularly develop new methods for bypassing security controls, and red teamers must learn about these threats as they arise. This includes staying informed about the latest malware, zero-day exploits, and advanced persistent threat (APT) tactics.
- **Improve effectiveness**: Ongoing training ensures that red teamers can adapt to new tools, technologies, and environments. This increases the effectiveness of red team engagements by allowing the team to simulate more sophisticated attacks and explore new avenues for compromising systems.
- **Adapt to evolving technologies**: As organizations adopt new technologies, such as cloud services, containerization, and artificial intelligence, red teams must acquire the necessary skills to assess the security of these systems. Training in emerging technologies allows red teamers to understand potential weaknesses and attack vectors specific to these environments.

3.3.2 Certifications and Formal Training

Certifications and formal training programs provide structured learning paths for red team professionals to develop their skills. These programs are recognized industry-wide and help red teamers validate their expertise in various areas of offensive security. Some of the most relevant certifications and training programs for red teamers include:

Offensive Security Certified Professional (OSCP): One of the most respected certifications in offensive security, the OSCP emphasizes hands-on penetration testing and exploitation skills. Earning this certification requires red teamers to demonstrate their ability to identify and exploit vulnerabilities in real-world systems.

Certified Red Team Professional (CRTP): This certification focuses specifically on red team operations, covering areas such as Active Directory exploitation, lateral movement, and privilege escalation. The CRTP provides practical, hands-on training for red teamers looking to advance their expertise in simulating real-world attacks.

GIAC Penetration Tester (GPEN): GPEN certification is geared toward penetration testing but provides red teamers with a solid foundation in conducting in-depth security assessments. The certification covers topics such as reconnaissance, vulnerability scanning, exploitation, and reporting.

CREST Registered Penetration Tester (CRT): The CRT certification is recognized globally and covers various aspects of penetration testing and red team operations. It focuses on hands-on skills in network, web application, and wireless security testing, as well as exploitation techniques.

Advanced Red Team Training Programs: In addition to certifications, many organizations offer specialized red team training courses. For example, the SANS Institute offers courses like SEC564: Red Team Operations and SEC760: Advanced Exploit Development, which focus on advanced offensive security tactics and red team-specific methodologies.

3.3.3 Hands-On Labs and Simulations

Practical, hands-on experience is vital for red teamers to refine their technical skills. Many training platforms offer simulated environments where red team members can practice exploiting vulnerabilities and testing different attack techniques without the risks associated with real-world engagements.

Capture the Flag (CTF) Competitions: CTF events challenge participants to solve security-related puzzles, identify vulnerabilities, and exploit systems in a competitive environment. These competitions provide an excellent opportunity for red teamers to practice real-world attack techniques, from web application exploitation to network security testing. Many organizations, such as DEF CON and Hack The Box, host regular CTF challenges.

Red Team Labs: Red teamers benefit from access to labs that simulate realistic network environments. Platforms like Offensive Security's Proving Grounds, TryHackMe, and RangeForce offer hands-on labs that allow red teamers to practice reconnaissance, exploitation, and post-exploitation techniques in controlled settings. These labs often simulate corporate networks, cloud environments, and various defense mechanisms that red teamers must overcome.

Adversary Emulation Platforms: Some platforms are specifically designed to simulate advanced persistent threats (APTs) and other real-world adversaries. These include tools like MITRE ATT&CK Evaluations and CALDERA, which allow red teams to practice emulating specific threat actors' tactics, techniques, and procedures (TTPs). Red teamers can use these platforms to sharpen their skills in evading detection, lateral movement, and data exfiltration.

Physical Security Testing Labs: Red teams that conduct physical security testing can benefit from training labs that replicate real-world physical environments. These labs may include mock data centers, offices, or secure facilities where red teamers can practice bypassing locks, tailgating, and other physical attack techniques.

3.3.4 Mentorship and Knowledge Sharing

Mentorship plays a crucial role in the development of red team professionals. Experienced red teamers can offer guidance, share insights, and provide valuable feedback to junior team members. Mentorship helps build confidence, accelerates skill development, and fosters a collaborative learning environment.

Internal Knowledge Sharing: Red teams can benefit from fostering a culture of continuous learning within the organization. This includes regular knowledge-sharing sessions, where team members present on new tools, techniques, or recent case studies. By collaborating and sharing experiences, red teamers can stay informed about the latest trends in offensive security and improve the team's overall effectiveness.

Cross-Training with Blue Teams: Red teams can also learn from defensive security teams (blue teams) by participating in joint exercises. This includes purple teaming, where red and blue teams collaborate to test and refine security defenses in real time. Red teamers gain valuable insights into how defensive measures are implemented and how they can improve their attack techniques to bypass those measures.

Participation in the Security Community: Active participation in the broader security community, including attending conferences, contributing to open-source projects, and collaborating with other security professionals, helps red teamers stay connected to the latest developments in the field. Conferences such as Black Hat, DEF CON, and BSides offer opportunities to learn from industry leaders and share experiences with peers.

3.3.5 Research and Development (R&D)

To stay on the cutting edge of offensive security, red teams should invest in research and development (R&D) efforts. This involves exploring new attack vectors, discovering vulnerabilities, and developing custom tools that can be used in future engagements.

Exploit Research: Red teamers should regularly explore new exploits and vulnerabilities, whether by reverse-engineering software or analyzing recent security advisories. By staying ahead of the curve, red teams can develop new attack techniques that mimic the behavior of advanced threat actors.

Tool Development: Red teams benefit from creating their own tools or enhancing existing ones to address specific needs during engagements. This includes developing scripts for automating tasks, writing custom exploits, or modifying open-source tools to better evade detection.

Collaboration with Academia: Some red teams collaborate with academic institutions to stay informed about cutting-edge research in areas such as malware development, artificial intelligence in security, and cryptography. By leveraging academic research, red teams can explore innovative approaches to offensive security.

3.3.6 Staying Updated on the Threat Landscape

Understanding the latest trends in the threat landscape is essential for red teamers to remain relevant. Threat intelligence feeds, industry reports, and security blogs are useful resources for keeping up with emerging threats and techniques used by attackers.

Threat Intelligence Feeds: Subscribing to threat intelligence platforms, such as Recorded Future, CrowdStrike, or FireEye, helps red teamers stay informed about the latest malware campaigns, phishing trends, and other cyber threats. This allows them to simulate up-to-date attack techniques during engagements.

Security Blogs and Reports: Reading blogs and reports from well-respected security researchers and organizations can provide red teamers with insights into emerging vulnerabilities, new attack tools, and real-world case studies of significant breaches. Websites such as KrebsOnSecurity, The Hacker News, and the MITRE ATT&CK framework are valuable resources.

Continuous training and development are crucial for red team professionals to remain effective in an ever-evolving threat landscape. Through certifications, hands-on labs, mentorship, and staying updated on the latest trends, red teamers can hone their skills and enhance their ability to simulate real-world attacks. By prioritizing education and knowledge-sharing within their teams, red teams can ensure they are well-equipped to help organizations identify and mitigate their security vulnerabilities.

Chapter 4: Red Team Methodologies and Frameworks

In this chapter, we explore the various methodologies and frameworks that guide red team operations, providing a structured approach to security testing. Understanding these frameworks is essential for effectively simulating adversarial behavior and aligning red team activities with organizational objectives. We will begin by introducing well-established frameworks, such as MITRE ATT&CK and NIST, discussing their significance in helping teams categorize and analyze attack techniques. Next, we will examine how to select the right methodology based on the specific needs and goals of an organization, taking into consideration factors like risk tolerance and compliance requirements. Additionally, this chapter will cover the integration of red teaming into an organization's overall security program, illustrating how to collaborate with blue teams and leverage insights gained from red team engagements. By the end of this chapter, readers will have a solid grasp of the methodologies and frameworks available to them, enabling them to conduct effective and meaningful red team exercises that drive real improvements in security.

4.1 Overview of Common Frameworks

In the field of red team operations, frameworks provide structured methodologies and best practices that guide teams in conducting effective security assessments. These frameworks not only help red teams organize their approach but also ensure that their tactics and techniques are aligned with real-world threats and industry standards. In this section, we will explore some of the most widely used red teaming frameworks that provide a solid foundation for planning, executing, and evaluating red team engagements.

4.1.1 MITRE ATT&CK Framework

The MITRE ATT&CK framework is one of the most comprehensive and widely adopted models for understanding and categorizing adversarial tactics, techniques, and procedures (TTPs). It provides a detailed matrix that maps out how real-world adversaries operate, from initial access to exfiltration and impact. The ATT&CK framework focuses on post-compromise behaviors and helps red teams emulate advanced threat actors by following similar techniques.

Key features of the MITRE ATT&CK framework include:

Adversary Tactics and Techniques: The framework organizes attack activities into tactics (goals) and techniques (methods). Tactics represent the objectives an attacker is trying to achieve (e.g., privilege escalation, persistence), while techniques describe the specific methods used to achieve these goals (e.g., credential dumping, lateral movement).

Threat Actor Emulation: By aligning red team operations with the ATT&CK matrix, teams can simulate the behaviors of advanced persistent threats (APTs) and other sophisticated adversaries. This helps organizations test their defenses against realistic, targeted attacks.

Coverage and Gaps: Using ATT&CK, red teams can assess which areas of the organization's defenses are vulnerable to specific techniques. It also helps identify gaps in detection and response capabilities by mapping red team activities against the ATT&CK framework's matrix.

4.1.2 Lockheed Martin Cyber Kill Chain

The Cyber Kill Chain, developed by Lockheed Martin, is a model that outlines the phases of a cyberattack, from the initial reconnaissance phase to the final objective of data exfiltration or system compromise. Originally designed for defending against advanced cyber threats, the Cyber Kill Chain is also a valuable tool for red teamers to structure their engagements and mirror how attackers move through different stages of an attack.

The seven phases of the Cyber Kill Chain include:

Reconnaissance: Attackers gather information about the target, such as network details, open ports, or employee information. Red teams mimic this stage by conducting OSINT (open-source intelligence) and network scanning.

Weaponization: In this phase, attackers create the malware or exploit needed to breach the target's defenses. Red teams develop payloads, custom malware, or phishing emails to initiate the attack.

Delivery: The attacker delivers the weaponized payload to the victim, often through phishing, malicious attachments, or drive-by downloads. Red teams execute this phase by delivering the payload using similar methods.

Exploitation: Exploiting vulnerabilities in systems, applications, or user behaviors allows attackers to gain a foothold. Red teams simulate this by exploiting the identified weaknesses.

Installation: Malware or backdoors are installed to maintain persistence within the system. Red teams emulate this by installing backdoors or using legitimate software to maintain access.

Command and Control (C2): Attackers establish communication channels with compromised systems to control and manipulate them. Red teams often set up C2 servers to simulate adversary command and control.

Actions on Objectives: Finally, attackers take action to achieve their goals, such as data theft, system disruption, or further lateral movement. Red teams mimic this by attempting to steal sensitive data or disrupt critical systems.

By following the phases of the Cyber Kill Chain, red teams can provide a structured and methodical approach to their engagements, ensuring all attack phases are covered.

4.1.3 NIST Special Publication 800-53 (Security and Privacy Controls)

The National Institute of Standards and Technology (NIST) provides comprehensive guidelines for security and privacy controls in NIST SP 800-53. While primarily a defense-oriented framework, red teams can use these controls to guide their testing and assessment processes, ensuring that their operations align with the latest federal standards for cybersecurity.

Some of the relevant NIST SP 800-53 controls for red team operations include:

Access Control (AC): Testing an organization's ability to manage who has access to systems and data. Red teams can focus on bypassing access control mechanisms to gain unauthorized access to critical assets.

Incident Response (IR): Evaluating how well an organization detects and responds to an attack. Red teams can test an organization's incident response capabilities by simulating various attack scenarios.

System and Communications Protection (SC): Red teams can test the security of communication channels, such as encrypted traffic and firewalls, to identify vulnerabilities that attackers could exploit.

By leveraging NIST SP 800-53 controls during red team engagements, teams ensure that they align their assessments with widely recognized security standards, which is particularly useful for organizations in regulated industries.

4.1.4 Red Teaming Maturity Models (RTMM)

Red Teaming Maturity Models (RTMM) are frameworks that measure an organization's maturity in terms of red team capabilities and effectiveness. These models provide a roadmap for organizations to gradually improve their red teaming efforts by advancing through various levels of maturity.

Typical stages in a Red Teaming Maturity Model include:

Initial Stage: Organizations at this level have limited or no red team capabilities. Security testing is often ad-hoc, and red team engagements may be sporadic or outsourced.

Defined Stage: At this stage, organizations have formalized red team processes and a dedicated red team. Engagements are planned, structured, and executed with a focus on improving security posture.

Integrated Stage: Red team operations are fully integrated with other security functions, such as blue teams and incident response teams (purple teaming). Continuous testing, feedback loops, and collaboration help improve the organization's overall security.

Adaptive Stage: At the highest level of maturity, red team operations are dynamic and adaptive. The red team is capable of simulating advanced and emerging threats, and their operations contribute to a continuous cycle of improvement across the organization.

4.1.5 OWASP (Open Web Application Security Project)

For organizations that prioritize web application security, the OWASP Top 10 is a widely recognized framework for identifying and addressing the most critical security risks to web applications. Red teams use OWASP as a guide to test web applications for common vulnerabilities and to simulate real-world attacks.

Key OWASP Top 10 vulnerabilities include:

Injection Attacks: Red teams test for SQL injection, command injection, and other types of injection flaws that allow attackers to manipulate systems or databases.

Cross-Site Scripting (XSS): Red teams attempt to exploit vulnerabilities that enable malicious scripts to be executed in a user's browser.

Security Misconfigurations: Red teams assess web applications for configuration errors that could lead to security breaches, such as exposed administrative interfaces or overly permissive settings.

The OWASP framework helps red teams focus on testing the security of web applications, which are often high-value targets for attackers.

Frameworks like MITRE ATT&CK, the Cyber Kill Chain, NIST SP 800-53, and others provide essential structures that guide red teams in their operations. These frameworks help red teams simulate real-world threats, test defenses comprehensively, and provide valuable insights to improve an organization's security posture. By adhering to these frameworks, red teams can ensure their engagements are well-organized, relevant, and aligned with industry standards, maximizing the value they deliver to their clients or organizations.

4.2 Selecting the Right Approach

Choosing the right approach to red team operations is crucial for maximizing the effectiveness of an engagement and aligning the objectives with the organization's specific needs. The approach depends on factors such as the organization's security posture, risk tolerance, scope, and the type of assets being targeted. This section explores the key considerations when selecting the appropriate red team approach and discusses different types of engagements that can be tailored to meet an organization's goals.

4.2.1 Aligning Objectives with Organizational Goals

The first step in selecting the right red team approach is to ensure that the objectives of the engagement align with the organization's overall security strategy and risk management goals. Red team operations can serve a variety of purposes, including:

Testing Incident Response Capabilities: If the organization wants to assess how well its security team responds to a simulated attack, the red team can focus on designing scenarios that stress test detection and response mechanisms.

Identifying Gaps in Critical Assets Protection: Organizations with valuable data, intellectual property, or critical infrastructure may prioritize engagements that focus on protecting those high-value targets. The red team should tailor its approach to exploit vulnerabilities in the areas that are most important to the organization's operations.

Improving Overall Security Posture: For organizations looking for a more holistic assessment, the red team can conduct broader engagements that test network defenses, physical security, employee awareness, and application security.

By clearly defining the purpose of the red team exercise, the team can select an approach that delivers meaningful results and actionable insights. This ensures that the engagement is not only a technical test but also a strategic tool that contributes to the organization's security roadmap.

4.2.2 Choosing Between Covert vs. Overt Engagements

One of the key decisions in selecting the right approach is whether the red team operation should be covert (stealthy) or overt (transparent). Each approach offers unique benefits and should be chosen based on the organization's specific needs and desired outcomes.

Covert Red Team Engagements: In a covert engagement, the red team operates under the assumption that its activities should remain undetected by the organization's security teams, mimicking the behavior of real-world attackers. This approach provides a realistic test of how well the organization's defenses, monitoring systems, and incident response teams can detect and respond to a genuine threat.

Advantages: Covert engagements simulate real-world adversarial behavior and allow the organization to evaluate its security team's readiness without prior knowledge of the attack. This can help identify gaps in monitoring, response, and detection that may not be apparent in an overt scenario.

Challenges: Because the goal is to remain undetected, covert operations require a high level of sophistication, planning, and stealth. Additionally, there may be legal or ethical concerns if key stakeholders are not aware of the red team engagement.

Overt Red Team Engagements: In an overt engagement, the red team's activities are known by the organization's security personnel ahead of time. This approach focuses on collaboration and improving the defenses in real time, often in the context of a "purple team" exercise where red and blue teams work together.

Advantages: Overt engagements allow for continuous feedback between red and blue teams, fostering a learning environment where both sides can improve. This approach is particularly useful for organizations that are still developing their security operations and want to actively enhance their detection and defense mechanisms during the engagement.

Challenges: Because the blue team is aware of the red team's actions, this may not provide as realistic a test of incident response capabilities. The engagement may also be less focused on stealth tactics, and more on exposing and addressing vulnerabilities as they arise.

The decision between covert and overt engagements should be based on the maturity of the organization's security program and its specific objectives for the red team exercise. For organizations seeking to assess their real-world readiness, a covert approach may be ideal. On the other hand, for teams looking to collaborate and strengthen their defenses, an overt approach can provide valuable insights.

4.2.3 Tailoring Red Team Engagements by Scope and Focus

Red team operations can vary significantly in scope, from broad assessments of the organization's overall security posture to focused tests of specific areas such as physical security or social engineering defenses. When selecting the right approach, it's important to tailor the engagement to the organization's unique requirements.

Full-Scope Engagements: A full-scope red team operation tests an organization's defenses across multiple domains, including physical security, network infrastructure, application security, and employee awareness. This type of engagement provides a comprehensive view of the organization's vulnerabilities and how different layers of defense interact with each other.

Benefits: Full-scope engagements allow red teams to simulate highly realistic, multi-faceted attacks that test an organization's ability to detect and respond to a coordinated attack from multiple vectors. This approach is ideal for organizations looking for a thorough assessment of their overall security.

Considerations: Full-scope engagements require significant time and resources and may involve a longer preparation phase to accurately simulate complex attack scenarios. The scope also needs to be clearly defined to avoid overwhelming the organization's security teams with too many simultaneous tests.

Targeted Engagements: A more focused red team operation might concentrate on specific areas of concern, such as social engineering or physical security. Targeted engagements are particularly useful for organizations that have identified specific weaknesses or that want to test a particular aspect of their security program.

Benefits: Targeted engagements allow red teams to deep-dive into specific vulnerabilities and provide a detailed assessment of how well the organization's defenses hold up against a particular threat. This focused approach is more efficient and can yield quick, actionable results.

Considerations: While targeted engagements are efficient, they may not provide a comprehensive view of the organization's overall security posture. They should be used in combination with broader assessments to ensure no critical vulnerabilities are overlooked.

By carefully defining the scope of the engagement, red teams can focus on the most relevant areas of the organization's security program, ensuring that the approach is aligned with the organization's priorities and resources.

4.2.4 Considering Compliance and Industry Standards

Many organizations operate in industries with strict regulatory requirements, such as finance, healthcare, or government. When selecting the right red team approach, it's important to consider how the engagement will align with industry standards and compliance requirements. Red team engagements may be designed specifically to test an organization's ability to meet these standards and to identify any gaps in compliance.

Compliance-Driven Engagements: For organizations that need to meet specific regulatory requirements, such as PCI-DSS, HIPAA, or NIST standards, red team operations can be tailored to focus on areas of compliance. These engagements ensure that the organization is meeting its obligations in terms of security controls, incident response, and data protection.

Benefits: Compliance-driven red team operations help organizations address regulatory requirements while also improving security. By testing compliance-related controls, red teams provide valuable insights into whether the organization is prepared to meet audit requirements.

Considerations: While compliance-driven engagements ensure that organizations meet their legal and regulatory obligations, they should not be the sole focus of red team operations. Red teams should strive to go beyond compliance and identify security gaps that may not be covered by industry standards.

4.2.5 Adversary Emulation vs. Vulnerability Assessment

A final consideration in selecting the right approach is whether to conduct an adversary emulation exercise or a more traditional vulnerability assessment. Both approaches have their merits and should be selected based on the organization's goals.

Adversary Emulation: This approach focuses on simulating the tactics, techniques, and procedures (TTPs) used by specific threat actors. Red teams emulate known adversaries, such as nation-state actors or cybercriminal groups, to see how well the organization can defend against real-world threats.

Benefits: Adversary emulation provides the most realistic test of an organization's defenses, as it mirrors actual attack scenarios. This approach helps organizations prepare for threats that are specific to their industry or region.

Challenges: Adversary emulation requires a deep understanding of the threat actors being simulated, as well as access to tools and techniques used by these adversaries. It also involves more complex planning and coordination to accurately reflect the behavior of the chosen threat actors.

Vulnerability Assessment: In contrast, vulnerability assessments are broader exercises that focus on identifying weaknesses in an organization's systems, applications, or networks. The red team scans for vulnerabilities and exploits them to determine their impact.

Benefits: Vulnerability assessments are useful for identifying a wide range of potential weaknesses, making them ideal for organizations that want to improve their overall security posture.

Challenges: While valuable, vulnerability assessments may not fully replicate the behavior of advanced adversaries, and thus may not provide as realistic a test of the organization's defenses.

Selecting the right red team approach is a critical decision that should be based on the organization's goals, risk tolerance, scope, and compliance requirements. By aligning objectives with security priorities, choosing between covert and overt engagements, tailoring the scope, and selecting between adversary emulation and vulnerability assessment, organizations can ensure that red team operations deliver maximum value and actionable insights.

4.3 Integrating Red Teaming into Security Programs

Integrating red teaming into an organization's security program is essential for developing a robust cybersecurity posture. This integration not only enhances an organization's ability to identify and mitigate vulnerabilities but also fosters a culture of continuous improvement and collaboration between various security functions. In this section, we will explore key strategies for effectively incorporating red team operations into existing security frameworks and programs.

4.3.1 Establishing a Red Team Strategy

Before integrating red teaming into a security program, organizations should develop a clear strategy that outlines the goals, scope, and objectives of red team operations. This strategy should align with the organization's overall security goals and risk management policies.

Defining Objectives: Establish clear objectives for the red team, such as improving incident response capabilities, testing security controls, or simulating advanced persistent threats (APTs). These objectives will guide the focus of the red team and ensure that their efforts align with organizational priorities.

Assessing Risk: Evaluate the organization's risk landscape to identify high-value assets, critical infrastructures, and potential vulnerabilities. This assessment will help prioritize red team engagements and determine where to focus testing efforts for maximum impact.

Engagement Planning: Develop a plan for how red team engagements will be conducted, including frequency, scope, and coordination with other security teams. This plan should also outline the methodologies and frameworks that will be used during engagements, such as MITRE ATT&CK or the Cyber Kill Chain.

4.3.2 Collaboration with Blue Teams

One of the most effective ways to integrate red teaming into security programs is to foster collaboration between red and blue teams. This approach, often referred to as "purple teaming," encourages the sharing of insights, strategies, and lessons learned to enhance overall security effectiveness.

Continuous Feedback Loop: Establish a feedback mechanism where red team findings are shared with blue teams immediately after engagements. This allows blue teams to respond to vulnerabilities in real time, improving their detection and response capabilities.

Joint Exercises: Conduct joint exercises where red and blue teams work together to simulate attacks and defenses. These exercises provide hands-on experience and create opportunities for knowledge sharing. The collaboration helps blue teams understand red team tactics, making them better equipped to defend against similar real-world threats.

Developing Playbooks: Red and blue teams should work together to create incident response playbooks that detail how to respond to specific attack scenarios. These playbooks should be updated regularly based on insights gained from red team engagements.

4.3.3 Incorporating Red Teaming into Security Assessments

Red team operations should be viewed as an integral part of the organization's broader security assessments. By incorporating red teaming into regular security evaluations, organizations can ensure that their defenses are continuously tested and improved.

Periodic Red Team Engagements: Schedule regular red team assessments as part of the organization's security testing lifecycle. These assessments should be aligned with major changes in the environment, such as new system deployments or significant changes in the threat landscape.

Integration with Vulnerability Management: Red teams should collaborate with vulnerability management programs to ensure that findings from red team engagements feed into the vulnerability remediation process. This collaboration helps prioritize vulnerabilities based on the level of risk they pose to the organization.

Aligning with Compliance Requirements: Organizations that must adhere to regulatory requirements can integrate red team operations into their compliance programs. Red teams can assist in testing the effectiveness of security controls that are part of compliance frameworks, ensuring that organizations meet their obligations while also improving security.

4.3.4 Training and Development

A critical aspect of integrating red teaming into security programs is investing in the training and development of both red and blue teams. Continuous education ensures that team members stay up to date with the latest tactics, techniques, and best practices in cybersecurity.

Skill Development: Provide ongoing training and development opportunities for red team members to learn new attack techniques, tools, and methodologies. Similarly, blue team members should receive training on threat detection and response strategies based on the insights gained from red team engagements.

Cross-Training: Encourage cross-training between red and blue teams, where team members learn about each other's roles and responsibilities. This fosters a better understanding of the entire security landscape and enhances collaboration during engagements.

Certifications and Courses: Support team members in obtaining relevant certifications and attending training courses related to red teaming and cybersecurity. Certifications such as Certified Ethical Hacker (CEH), Offensive Security Certified Professional (OSCP), and Certified Red Team Professional (CRTP) can enhance team skills and credibility.

4.3.5 Leveraging Technology and Tools

To effectively integrate red teaming into security programs, organizations should leverage technology and tools that facilitate collaboration, automation, and reporting. These tools can streamline red team operations and enhance the effectiveness of security assessments.

Collaboration Platforms: Utilize collaboration platforms that allow red and blue teams to communicate in real time, share findings, and document lessons learned. Tools like Slack, Microsoft Teams, or specialized security platforms can enhance coordination and information sharing.

Automated Testing Tools: Incorporate automated testing tools that assist red teams in identifying vulnerabilities and conducting assessments more efficiently. Tools such as penetration testing frameworks, vulnerability scanners, and exploit development environments can enhance the effectiveness of red team engagements.

Reporting and Metrics: Implement reporting tools that allow red teams to document findings, track vulnerabilities, and measure the effectiveness of remediation efforts. Metrics should be defined to assess the impact of red team engagements on overall security posture.

4.3.6 Measuring Success and Continuous Improvement

Finally, it is essential to measure the success of red team integrations within security programs and continuously improve processes based on findings and feedback.

Establishing KPIs: Define key performance indicators (KPIs) to measure the effectiveness of red team operations. Metrics may include the number of vulnerabilities identified, the time taken to remediate findings, and the improvement in incident response times.

Post-Engagement Reviews: Conduct post-engagement reviews to evaluate the effectiveness of red team operations. These reviews should involve both red and blue teams and focus on discussing findings, lessons learned, and areas for improvement.

Iterative Improvements: Foster a culture of continuous improvement where red team engagements inform and refine security strategies, policies, and practices. Use insights from engagements to enhance detection capabilities, refine incident response processes, and improve security training programs.

Integrating red teaming into security programs is a multifaceted process that involves establishing a clear strategy, fostering collaboration, incorporating red teaming into assessments, and leveraging technology. By focusing on continuous improvement and collaboration between red and blue teams, organizations can create a dynamic security environment that enhances their overall cybersecurity posture. Ultimately, effective integration of red team operations enables organizations to proactively identify and mitigate vulnerabilities, preparing them to defend against real-world threats more effectively.

Chapter 5: Planning and Scoping Red Team Engagements

In this chapter, we delve into the critical process of planning and scoping red team engagements, which lays the foundation for successful security testing initiatives. Proper planning ensures that red team operations are aligned with organizational goals, legal requirements, and stakeholder expectations. We will begin by discussing how to define clear objectives and success criteria for engagements, emphasizing the importance of establishing what the organization hopes to achieve through red teaming efforts. Next, we will explore the legal and ethical considerations that must be taken into account to avoid potential liabilities and ensure responsible testing practices. Additionally, this chapter will highlight the significance of effective stakeholder communication, detailing how to manage expectations and foster a collaborative environment. By the conclusion of this chapter, readers will be equipped with the knowledge and tools necessary to effectively scope their red team engagements, ensuring that they are not only impactful but also conducted within a framework of accountability and transparency.

5.1 Defining Objectives and Success Criteria

Defining clear objectives and success criteria for red team engagements is a critical step in the planning process. By establishing these elements, organizations can ensure that their red team activities are aligned with their overall security goals and provide actionable insights that contribute to the improvement of their cybersecurity posture. This section discusses the importance of setting objectives and success criteria, how to develop them, and the impact they have on red team operations.

Importance of Defining Objectives

Objectives serve as the foundation for any red team engagement, guiding the scope, focus, and methodologies employed during the exercise. Clearly defined objectives help ensure that red team activities are purposeful and relevant to the organization's specific security needs. Here are several reasons why defining objectives is essential:

Alignment with Organizational Goals: Objectives should reflect the organization's overall security strategy and risk management priorities. By aligning red team objectives with broader business goals, organizations can ensure that the findings from red team activities have meaningful implications for their security posture.

Focus on Specific Outcomes: Clear objectives allow the red team to concentrate their efforts on specific areas of concern, whether that be testing incident response capabilities, assessing the effectiveness of security controls, or identifying vulnerabilities in critical assets. This focused approach enables teams to maximize the impact of their engagements.

Guiding the Scope of Engagements: Defining objectives helps establish the boundaries of red team operations, including what systems, applications, or processes will be tested. This clarity aids in resource allocation and helps prevent scope creep during engagements.

Measuring Success: Establishing objectives provides a basis for evaluating the success of red team engagements. By clearly articulating what success looks like, organizations can measure outcomes against these predefined criteria to assess the effectiveness of their security programs.

Developing Objectives

When developing objectives for red team engagements, organizations should consider several key factors to ensure that the objectives are relevant, achievable, and impactful:

Understand the Threat Landscape: Organizations should start by understanding the current threat landscape, including the types of threats they face, the tactics employed by adversaries, and the vulnerabilities that may be exploited. This understanding informs the development of objectives that are aligned with real-world risks.

Engage Stakeholders: Collaboration with key stakeholders, including executive leadership, security teams, and IT staff, is crucial in developing objectives that reflect organizational priorities. Engaging stakeholders ensures that objectives are relevant and that the red team's findings will resonate with decision-makers.

Prioritize Risks: Organizations should prioritize risks based on their potential impact and likelihood. Red team objectives should focus on high-risk areas that are critical to the organization's operations or that may expose sensitive data. This prioritization helps ensure that red team efforts are directed toward the most pressing security concerns.

Specificity and Measurability: Objectives should be specific, measurable, achievable, relevant, and time-bound (SMART). For example, rather than stating a broad objective like "improve security," a more specific objective would be "identify and exploit vulnerabilities in web applications within a three-week timeframe." This specificity allows for clearer evaluation of the engagement's success.

Establishing Success Criteria

In addition to defining objectives, it is equally important to establish success criteria that allow organizations to evaluate the outcomes of red team engagements. Success criteria are measurable benchmarks that help determine whether the objectives have been achieved. Here are some essential aspects to consider when establishing success criteria:

Quantifiable Metrics: Success criteria should include quantifiable metrics that provide clear indicators of performance. Metrics may include the number of vulnerabilities identified, the severity of those vulnerabilities, the time taken to detect and respond to simulated attacks, or the percentage of identified vulnerabilities that were remediated within a specified timeframe.

Performance Benchmarks: Establish performance benchmarks based on industry standards, past engagements, or organizational goals. For example, organizations might set a target for their incident response teams to identify and respond to a simulated breach within a certain time frame, such as 30 minutes.

Stakeholder Feedback: Incorporate qualitative success criteria that reflect the perspectives of stakeholders. Feedback from security personnel, executives, and other relevant parties can provide valuable insights into the perceived effectiveness of the red team engagement. For example, assessing whether security teams feel more prepared to respond to real threats post-engagement can be a key success indicator.

Continuous Improvement: Success criteria should not only focus on immediate outcomes but also consider the long-term impact of red team engagements on the organization's security posture. For instance, assessing the changes made to security policies, training programs, or incident response processes as a result of red team findings can provide a measure of ongoing improvement.

Evaluating Success and Lessons Learned

After a red team engagement, organizations should conduct a thorough evaluation to determine whether objectives were met and success criteria were achieved. This evaluation should involve:

Post-Engagement Review: A post-engagement review should be conducted with all relevant stakeholders, including red and blue team members, to discuss findings, successes, and areas for improvement. This collaborative approach promotes transparency and encourages the sharing of insights that can enhance future engagements.

Reporting Findings: A comprehensive report should be generated that summarizes the engagement's objectives, findings, and recommendations. This report serves as a valuable resource for stakeholders, providing actionable insights that can inform security strategies and improvements.

Tracking Improvements: Organizations should track the implementation of recommendations made during the engagement and monitor the effectiveness of those improvements over time. This tracking enables organizations to assess the lasting impact of red team activities on their overall security posture.

Defining clear objectives and success criteria is a fundamental component of effective red team operations. By establishing well-defined objectives that align with organizational goals and by developing measurable success criteria, organizations can ensure that their red team engagements are purposeful, relevant, and impactful. This approach not only enhances the effectiveness of red team activities but also contributes to the ongoing improvement of the organization's cybersecurity posture, ultimately leading to a stronger defense against evolving threats. Through careful planning and evaluation, red team engagements can provide valuable insights that inform security strategies, foster collaboration, and drive continuous improvement across the organization.

5.2 Legal and Ethical Considerations

When conducting red team operations, navigating the complex landscape of legal and ethical considerations is paramount. Red teaming involves simulating real-world attacks to test an organization's defenses, which inherently raises numerous legal and ethical issues. Understanding and addressing these concerns is crucial for ensuring that red team engagements are conducted responsibly, transparently, and within the bounds of the law. This section delves into the key legal and ethical considerations that organizations must take into account during red team operations.

Legal Considerations

Authorization and Consent:

- **Written Authorization**: Before initiating any red team engagement, obtaining explicit written authorization from the organization's leadership is essential. This authorization should clearly define the scope of the engagement, the systems and networks to be tested, and the specific actions that are permitted. This documentation serves as a legal safeguard for both the red team and the organization.
- **Scope Definition**: Clearly defining the scope of the engagement is critical to avoid legal repercussions. Unauthorized access to systems or data outside the agreed-upon scope can lead to legal liabilities, including potential civil or criminal charges.

Data Privacy Laws:

- **Compliance with Regulations**: Organizations must be aware of applicable data privacy laws and regulations, such as the General Data Protection Regulation (GDPR), the Health Insurance Portability and Accountability Act (HIPAA), or the California Consumer Privacy Act (CCPA). Red team operations should comply with these regulations, particularly when handling personal or sensitive data during testing.
- **Data Handling and Protection**: Proper protocols for data handling should be established to protect sensitive information. This includes ensuring that any data collected during the red team engagement is securely stored, anonymized when possible, and deleted or destroyed once the engagement is complete.

Intellectual Property Considerations:

Respecting IP Rights: Red teams must respect the intellectual property rights of the organization and third parties. Unauthorized use or exploitation of proprietary software, trade secrets, or other intellectual property during testing can lead to legal disputes and damage the organization's reputation.

Liability and Insurance:

- **Understanding Liability Risks**: Organizations should assess potential liability risks associated with red team engagements. This includes understanding the legal implications of any damage or disruption caused during testing, whether intentional or unintentional.

- **Insurance Coverage**: Securing appropriate liability insurance can help mitigate financial risks associated with red team operations. Organizations may consider cybersecurity insurance that covers incidents arising from red team engagements, including data breaches or system outages.

Reporting Obligations:

Disclosure of Findings: If a red team engagement uncovers vulnerabilities or breaches that require notification to regulatory authorities or affected individuals, organizations must understand their reporting obligations. Adhering to these requirements is critical for maintaining compliance and avoiding penalties.

Ethical Considerations

Responsible Disclosure:

- **Communication of Findings**: Ethical red teaming involves responsibly disclosing findings to the appropriate stakeholders within the organization. Vulnerabilities and weaknesses identified during testing should be communicated in a clear and constructive manner, allowing the organization to take necessary remediation actions.
- **Timing of Disclosure**: Consideration should be given to the timing of disclosures. Immediate reporting of critical vulnerabilities is essential, while less severe findings can be addressed in a structured debriefing after the engagement.

Adherence to Ethical Standards:

- **Professional Conduct**: Red team members should adhere to professional ethical standards throughout the engagement. This includes treating all personnel with respect, maintaining confidentiality, and acting with integrity at all times.
- **Avoiding Harm**: Red team operations should prioritize avoiding harm to individuals, systems, and the organization as a whole. Testing should be conducted in a manner that minimizes disruption and risk, ensuring that operations can continue without significant impact.

Transparency and Accountability:

- **Clear Communication**: Transparency in communication with stakeholders is vital. Organizations should be informed about the goals, methods, and potential risks associated with red team engagements. This transparency builds trust and fosters a collaborative environment.
- **Accountability for Actions**: Red team members should take responsibility for their actions during engagements. Establishing clear guidelines for ethical behavior and accountability can help mitigate risks and ensure that red team activities align with organizational values.

Cultural Sensitivity:

- **Awareness of Organizational Culture**: Red team members should be sensitive to the organizational culture and dynamics. Understanding the unique challenges and concerns of the organization can inform the approach taken during testing and enhance the effectiveness of the engagement.
- **Inclusivity and Diversity**: Promoting inclusivity and diversity within red team operations can lead to more comprehensive assessments. Engaging individuals from diverse backgrounds can provide varied perspectives on vulnerabilities and security practices, ultimately strengthening the security posture.

Continuous Education and Training:

- **Staying Informed**: Red team members should engage in continuous education and training to stay informed about the latest legal, ethical, and technical developments in cybersecurity. This commitment to learning enhances their effectiveness and helps ensure compliance with evolving legal and ethical standards.
- **Ethics Training**: Incorporating ethics training into red team development programs can reinforce the importance of ethical behavior and decision-making. Training should cover legal obligations, ethical dilemmas, and best practices for responsible red teaming.

Legal and ethical considerations are foundational elements of successful red team operations. By prioritizing authorization, compliance with data privacy laws, and responsible disclosure practices, organizations can mitigate legal risks and foster a culture of ethical behavior within their red team engagements. Clear guidelines and frameworks for red teaming not only protect the organization but also enhance the effectiveness of the testing process, ultimately contributing to a more robust cybersecurity posture. As the threat landscape continues to evolve, organizations must remain vigilant in addressing these considerations to ensure that their red team operations are conducted responsibly, transparently, and in alignment with both legal and ethical standards.

5.3 Stakeholder Communication

Effective stakeholder communication is a cornerstone of successful red team operations. In the realm of cybersecurity, where threats are constantly evolving and the landscape is often complex, clear and structured communication is vital. Stakeholders—ranging from executives and security teams to IT personnel and regulatory bodies—need to be informed, engaged, and aligned with the goals of red team activities. This section explores the importance of stakeholder communication, strategies for effective communication, and best practices for ensuring that all relevant parties are informed and engaged throughout the red team lifecycle.

Importance of Stakeholder Communication

Alignment of Objectives:

- **Shared Goals**: Clear communication helps ensure that red team objectives align with the organization's broader security strategy. By keeping stakeholders informed, the red team can tailor its approach to meet the specific needs and expectations of the organization.
- **Understanding Priorities**: Engaging with stakeholders allows the red team to understand the organization's priorities and risk appetite. This knowledge enables the team to focus their efforts on high-impact areas that matter most to the organization.

Building Trust:

- **Transparency**: Open communication fosters trust between the red team and stakeholders. By transparently sharing plans, methodologies, and findings, the red team demonstrates professionalism and integrity, reinforcing stakeholders' confidence in their work.
- **Mitigating Concerns**: Stakeholders may have concerns regarding potential disruptions or misunderstandings during red team engagements. By proactively addressing these concerns through clear communication, the red team can alleviate apprehensions and build stronger relationships.

Facilitating Collaboration:

- **Cross-Functional Engagement**: Red team operations often involve collaboration with various teams, including blue teams, incident response, and IT departments. Effective communication ensures that all parties are aware of their roles, responsibilities, and how they can contribute to the success of the engagement.
- **Feedback Loop**: Establishing a communication framework enables the red team to gather feedback from stakeholders during and after engagements. This feedback can inform future operations and enhance the overall effectiveness of red team efforts.

Ensuring Accountability:

- **Documented Communication**: Keeping a record of communications with stakeholders ensures accountability for decisions made and actions taken during red team engagements. This documentation can be useful for future reference, audits, or incident investigations.
- **Clear Expectations**: By communicating expectations clearly, the red team can help stakeholders understand the purpose, scope, and potential impact of the engagement. This clarity supports effective coordination and execution of red team activities.

Strategies for Effective Stakeholder Communication

Identify Key Stakeholders:

- **Mapping Stakeholders**: Begin by identifying all relevant stakeholders, including executive leadership, security teams, IT personnel, and legal advisors. Understanding who needs to be involved in the communication process is crucial for developing tailored messages.
- **Segmenting Stakeholders**: Different stakeholders may have varying levels of technical knowledge and different interests. Segment stakeholders based on their roles, expertise, and needs to tailor communication effectively.

Establish Communication Channels:

- **Preferred Channels**: Determine the preferred communication channels for different stakeholders. Options may include email updates, meetings, reports, and collaborative tools like Slack or Microsoft Teams.

- **Regular Updates**: Schedule regular check-ins or updates to keep stakeholders informed of progress, findings, and any emerging issues. Consistency in communication helps build trust and keeps stakeholders engaged.

Define Communication Objectives:

- **Clarity of Purpose**: Each communication should have a clear objective, whether it's to inform stakeholders about an upcoming engagement, share findings from a completed assessment, or solicit feedback. Clearly defining objectives helps keep communications focused and effective.
- **Tailored Messaging**: Craft messages that resonate with the specific audience. For example, executive summaries should focus on high-level insights and strategic implications, while technical teams may require more detailed technical findings.

Develop Comprehensive Reporting:

- **Engagement Reports**: After each red team engagement, produce a comprehensive report detailing the objectives, methodologies, findings, and recommendations. These reports serve as key communication tools for stakeholders and provide a valuable resource for ongoing security improvements.
- **Executive Summaries**: Accompany detailed reports with executive summaries that highlight key findings, recommendations, and strategic insights. These summaries should be concise and easily digestible for non-technical stakeholders.

Encourage Two-Way Communication:

- **Soliciting Feedback**: Actively solicit feedback from stakeholders throughout the engagement process. This feedback can provide valuable insights and perspectives that can enhance the effectiveness of red team operations.
- **Open Dialogue**: Foster an environment where stakeholders feel comfortable asking questions or expressing concerns. Open dialogue promotes collaboration and allows for the identification of potential challenges early on.

Best Practices for Stakeholder Communication

Establish a Communication Plan:

- **Documentation**: Create a communication plan that outlines how information will be shared with stakeholders throughout the red team engagement. This plan should include communication objectives, key messages, channels, and timelines.
- **Role Assignments**: Assign specific team members to manage stakeholder communication. This ensures accountability and consistency in messaging.

Utilize Visual Aids:

- **Data Visualization**: Use charts, graphs, and other visual aids to present complex findings in a clear and understandable manner. Visual representations can enhance stakeholder comprehension and retention of key information.
- **Infographics**: Consider creating infographics that summarize key findings and recommendations. These can be shared in presentations or as standalone documents to facilitate quick understanding.

Be Clear and Concise:

- **Avoid Jargon**: Use plain language and avoid technical jargon when communicating with non-technical stakeholders. Clear and concise messaging enhances understanding and ensures that critical information is conveyed effectively.
- **Focus on Key Takeaways**: Highlight the most important findings and recommendations, ensuring that stakeholders can grasp the key messages without being overwhelmed by excessive detail.

Follow Up:

- **Post-Engagement Debrief**: Schedule debriefing sessions with stakeholders after the completion of red team engagements. These sessions provide an opportunity to discuss findings, answer questions, and outline next steps for remediation and improvement.
- **Ongoing Engagement**: Continue to engage stakeholders beyond individual red team engagements. Regular follow-ups on the implementation of recommendations and updates on the organization's security posture reinforce the value of red team operations.

Document Communication Outcomes:

- **Tracking Decisions**: Keep a record of important decisions made during communications with stakeholders. This documentation can serve as a reference for future engagements and help track the organization's progress n addressing identified vulnerabilities.
- **Feedback Documentation**: Document stakeholder feedback and concerns to inform future red team operations. Understanding past stakeholder perspectives can help shape more effective communication strategies moving forward.

Effective stakeholder communication is essential for the success of red team operations. By aligning objectives, building trust, facilitating collaboration, and ensuring accountability, organizations can maximize the impact of their red team engagements. Employing strategic communication practices, developing comprehensive reporting, and encouraging two-way communication will foster a culture of transparency and continuous improvement. As the cybersecurity landscape continues to evolve, maintaining open and effective communication with stakeholders will be crucial for ensuring that red team operations contribute meaningfully to the organization's overall security posture. Ultimately, prioritizing stakeholder communication enhances the effectiveness of red team activities and strengthens the organization's defenses against evolving threats.

Chapter 6: Reconnaissance Techniques

In this chapter, we examine the vital phase of reconnaissance, which serves as the foundation for any successful red team engagement. Reconnaissance involves gathering critical information about a target organization to identify potential vulnerabilities and weaknesses before executing an attack. We will begin by differentiating between passive and active reconnaissance techniques, highlighting their respective advantages and the scenarios in which each method is most effective. The chapter will delve into the world of Open Source Intelligence (OSINT), showcasing various tools and techniques for collecting publicly available data, such as social media profiles, domain registrations, and network infrastructure details. Additionally, we will explore the importance of context in reconnaissance, emphasizing how understanding the target's environment can enhance the effectiveness of subsequent phases in the red teaming process. By the end of this chapter, readers will have a comprehensive understanding of reconnaissance techniques and will be equipped with the skills to gather and analyze intelligence that will inform their attack strategies, ultimately increasing the chances of a successful engagement.

6.1 Passive vs. Active Reconnaissance

Reconnaissance is the first stage of any red team engagement, serving as the foundation for subsequent testing activities. During this phase, the red team gathers information about the target organization to identify vulnerabilities, assess potential attack vectors, and formulate an effective attack strategy. Reconnaissance can be categorized into two primary types: passive reconnaissance and active reconnaissance. Understanding the differences between these two approaches is crucial for effectively planning and executing red team operations.

Passive Reconnaissance

Passive reconnaissance involves gathering information about a target without directly interacting with the target systems or networks. This approach minimizes the risk of detection and is often used to collect preliminary data that can inform later stages of an attack. Here are key characteristics and techniques associated with passive reconnaissance:

Characteristics:

- **Non-Intrusive**: Passive reconnaissance does not involve direct engagement with the target. Instead, it relies on publicly available information and third-party sources.
- **Low Risk of Detection**: Since there is no direct interaction with the target, the risk of being detected or raising alarms is significantly lower compared to active reconnaissance.
- **Focus on Publicly Available Information**: Passive reconnaissance leverages open-source intelligence (OSINT), which includes data that can be accessed without any unauthorized access to systems.

Techniques:

- **Domain Name System (DNS) Queries**: Gathering information through DNS queries can provide insights into the target's domain structure, IP address ranges, and mail server configurations. Tools like nslookup and dig are commonly used for this purpose.
- **Social Media and Public Profiles**: Analyzing social media accounts, company websites, and employee profiles on platforms like LinkedIn can reveal valuable information about personnel, technologies used, and organizational structure.
- **Public Records and Registries**: Accessing public records, such as business registrations, permits, and legal filings, can yield insights into the organization's operations, assets, and partnerships.
- **Search Engines and Archiving Services**: Utilizing search engines (e.g., Google, Bing) and archiving services (e.g., the Wayback Machine) can help discover historical data, old website versions, and documents that may reveal vulnerabilities.

Advantages:

- **Stealth**: Passive reconnaissance allows red teams to gather information without alerting the target, making it an effective first step in the reconnaissance process.
- **Cost-Effective**: Since this approach relies on publicly available information, it often requires less time and resources compared to active methods.

Limitations:

- **Limited Scope**: Passive reconnaissance may not provide comprehensive insights into the target's internal systems and defenses, as it relies solely on external information.

- **Information Age Sensitivity**: Publicly available information can be outdated or incomplete, which may lead to gaps in the red team's understanding of the target.

Active Reconnaissance

Active reconnaissance, in contrast, involves direct interaction with the target's systems or networks to gather information. This approach is more intrusive and carries a higher risk of detection, but it often yields more detailed and specific information about the target's vulnerabilities and defenses. Below are key characteristics and techniques associated with active reconnaissance:

Characteristics:

- **Intrusive**: Active reconnaissance involves sending probes, queries, or other requests to the target, which can raise alerts and increase the likelihood of detection.
- **Detailed Information Gathering**: This approach allows red teams to obtain specific details about the target's systems, configurations, and potential vulnerabilities.
- **Real-Time Data Collection**: Active reconnaissance can provide real-time information that reflects the current state of the target's defenses.

Techniques:

- **Port Scanning**: Tools such as Nmap or Netcat can be used to scan the target's IP addresses to identify open ports and services running on those ports. This information is crucial for determining potential entry points for attacks.
- **Network Mapping**: Active reconnaissance may involve creating a map of the target's network architecture, identifying devices, IP addresses, and the relationships between them.
- **Vulnerability Scanning**: Automated tools like Nessus or OpenVAS can be employed to scan the target's systems for known vulnerabilities. This allows red teams to identify weaknesses that could be exploited.
- **Service Enumeration**: Once open ports and services are identified, red teams can enumerate specific service versions, configurations, and potential misconfigurations that may be targeted in an attack.

Advantages:

- **Comprehensive Data**: Active reconnaissance often provides more in-depth and actionable information about the target's security posture, making it easier to identify specific vulnerabilities.
- **Current Insights**: Active techniques can yield real-time data, reflecting the current state of the target's defenses and allowing for timely attack planning.

Limitations:

- **Risk of Detection**: The intrusive nature of active reconnaissance increases the likelihood of detection by security monitoring systems. This can trigger alerts and lead to a response from the target's security team.
- **Potential for Escalation**: If not conducted carefully, active reconnaissance can unintentionally disrupt services or lead to unintended consequences, including legal ramifications.

Choosing the Right Approach

The choice between passive and active reconnaissance depends on several factors, including the goals of the red team engagement, the risk tolerance of the organization, and the potential impact of detection. Here are some considerations for selecting the appropriate reconnaissance strategy:

Engagement Objectives: If the goal is to gather preliminary information without attracting attention, passive reconnaissance is the preferred approach. However, if the objective is to gain deeper insights into specific systems or vulnerabilities, active reconnaissance may be necessary.

Risk Assessment: Organizations should evaluate their risk appetite when deciding on the reconnaissance method. If the risks of detection outweigh the benefits of detailed information, passive methods may be favored.

Stage of Engagement: In the initial phases of a red team engagement, passive reconnaissance is often used to lay the groundwork for more intrusive active reconnaissance in later stages. A phased approach can help balance the need for information with the need for stealth.

Legal and Ethical Considerations: Organizations must also consider legal and ethical implications when selecting reconnaissance methods. Active reconnaissance may require additional legal authorizations or agreements, especially if it involves probing production systems.

Both passive and active reconnaissance play essential roles in the red team lifecycle, each offering distinct advantages and challenges. Passive reconnaissance provides a stealthy means of gathering publicly available information, while active reconnaissance allows for more in-depth analysis of target systems. Understanding the differences between these two approaches is crucial for red teams to effectively plan their engagements, minimize risks, and maximize the impact of their testing efforts. By carefully selecting the appropriate reconnaissance techniques, red teams can develop a comprehensive understanding of their targets, ultimately leading to more successful assessments and recommendations for improving cybersecurity posture.

6.2 Open Source Intelligence (OSINT) Gathering

Open Source Intelligence (OSINT) refers to the process of collecting, analyzing, and utilizing information that is publicly available and accessible. In the context of cybersecurity and red teaming, OSINT plays a crucial role in reconnaissance, helping teams gather vital data about potential targets without engaging in intrusive activities. This chapter delves into the significance of OSINT gathering, various methods for collecting OSINT, tools commonly used in the process, and best practices for ensuring effective and ethical OSINT practices.

Significance of OSINT Gathering

Foundation for Cyber Operations:

- OSINT serves as the groundwork for subsequent stages of a red team engagement. It provides critical insights into the target's infrastructure, personnel, and security posture, allowing red teams to devise tailored attack strategies.
- By identifying potential vulnerabilities and entry points, red teams can focus their efforts on high-risk areas, making their engagements more effective and efficient.

Cost-Effective Approach:

- Gathering OSINT is generally more cost-effective than employing other intelligence-gathering methods, such as paid sources or proprietary databases. It allows red teams to leverage publicly available resources without incurring significant expenses.
- Since OSINT relies on existing data, red teams can save time and resources that would otherwise be spent on more invasive reconnaissance techniques.

Stealthy Information Gathering:

- OSINT gathering is typically non-intrusive, posing minimal risk of detection. This stealthiness is crucial in maintaining operational security and avoiding triggering alerts within the target organization.
- By utilizing publicly available information, red teams can gather intelligence without raising suspicion or alerting the target's security team.

Real-Time Insights:

- OSINT can provide real-time insights into an organization's activities, technologies, and personnel. This timeliness is particularly valuable in a rapidly changing threat landscape, allowing red teams to adapt their strategies as necessary.
- Staying informed about current events and developments related to the target organization can help red teams identify emerging vulnerabilities and attack vectors.

Methods of OSINT Gathering

Web Scraping:

- Web scraping involves extracting information from websites using automated tools or scripts. This method can gather data from social media platforms, forums, blogs, and corporate websites.
- Tools like Beautiful Soup and Scrapy can automate the extraction process, enabling red teams to collect large volumes of data efficiently.

Search Engines:

- Utilizing search engines is a fundamental method of OSINT gathering. Red teams can leverage advanced search operators (e.g., Google Dorks) to locate specific information about the target.
- Search engines can reveal sensitive information that may be inadvertently exposed online, such as email addresses, documents, and system configurations.

Social Media Analysis:

- Social media platforms like LinkedIn, Twitter, and Facebook provide rich sources of information about individuals and organizations. Red teams can analyze profiles, posts, and interactions to gather insights into personnel, organizational structure, and technologies used.
- Monitoring social media can also help identify potential insider threats or key personnel who may be targeted for social engineering attacks.

WHOIS Lookups:

- WHOIS databases provide information about domain registrations, including ownership details, contact information, and domain expiration dates. This data can help red teams identify the individuals or organizations behind a target domain.
- Tools like WHOIS.net and DomainTools can streamline this process, allowing red teams to gather critical information about a target's digital presence.

Public Records and Databases:

- Many jurisdictions maintain public records that can provide valuable insights into organizations. These records may include business registrations, legal filings, and property ownership documents.
- By searching through these databases, red teams can uncover information about the target's operations, financial status, and partnerships.

Online Forums and Communities:

- Online forums, discussion boards, and community sites can be treasure troves of information. Red teams can monitor discussions related to the target organization or industry to identify vulnerabilities, threats, and trends.
- Engaging with community members (anonymously) can yield valuable intelligence and insider knowledge about the target.

Tools for OSINT Gathering

Maltego:

Maltego is a powerful OSINT tool that visualizes relationships and connections between various entities. It allows red teams to conduct link analysis, uncovering hidden connections between domains, emails, and social media profiles.

Recon-ng:

Recon-ng is a web reconnaissance framework that provides a modular approach to gathering OSINT. It offers various modules for domain reconnaissance, social media analysis, and geolocation, making it a versatile tool for red teams.

TheHarvester:

TheHarvester is an OSINT tool designed to collect email addresses and subdomain names from public sources. It can scrape information from search engines and social media platforms, providing red teams with valuable data.

OSINT Framework:

The OSINT Framework is a collection of online resources and tools categorized by data type. It helps red teams identify relevant tools for specific OSINT gathering tasks, streamlining the research process.

Shodan:

Shodan is a search engine for internet-connected devices. Red teams can use it to identify devices, services, and vulnerabilities associated with the target organization's infrastructure.

Best Practices for OSINT Gathering

Define Clear Objectives:

Before beginning OSINT gathering, red teams should define clear objectives and specific information requirements. This focus ensures that the gathering process remains targeted and efficient.

Maintain Ethical Standards:

- Ethical considerations should guide OSINT gathering activities. Red teams must respect privacy and legal boundaries, avoiding unauthorized access to sensitive information.
- It is essential to avoid exploiting any discovered vulnerabilities or engaging in illegal activities during the OSINT gathering process.

Verify Information Sources:

- Not all publicly available information is accurate or reliable. Red teams should cross-reference information from multiple sources to verify its accuracy before including it in their analysis.
- Prioritize reputable sources, and be wary of unverified claims or rumors that may lead to misinformation.

Document Findings:

- Red teams should document all OSINT gathering activities, including sources, methods, and findings. This documentation serves as a reference for future engagements and aids in building a comprehensive intelligence profile of the target.
- Clear documentation also facilitates reporting to stakeholders and ensures accountability.

Stay Updated:

- The information landscape is dynamic, and new data is constantly emerging. Red teams should regularly update their OSINT gathering efforts to stay informed about changes related to the target organization, industry trends, and evolving threats.
- Subscribe to relevant news sources, forums, and alerts to receive timely updates on potential threats or vulnerabilities.

Leverage Collaboration:

- Red teams can benefit from collaborating with other teams, such as threat intelligence analysts or incident response teams. Sharing insights and findings can enhance the overall understanding of the target's threat landscape.
- Engaging in community discussions and knowledge-sharing forums can also yield valuable insights and best practices for OSINT gathering.

Open Source Intelligence (OSINT) gathering is a fundamental aspect of red team operations, providing valuable insights that inform attack strategies and vulnerability assessments. By leveraging publicly available information, red teams can gather critical intelligence while minimizing the risks associated with intrusive reconnaissance methods. Employing various techniques and tools, along with adhering to best practices, enhances the effectiveness and ethical considerations of OSINT gathering.

As the cyber threat landscape continues to evolve, OSINT will remain an essential component of red teaming, empowering organizations to proactively identify vulnerabilities and strengthen their cybersecurity posture.

6.3 Tools for Effective Reconnaissance

Reconnaissance is a critical phase in red team operations, allowing teams to gather information about their targets before executing any attacks. The effectiveness of this phase heavily relies on the tools used to collect, analyze, and organize the gathered intelligence. A wide range of tools, both open-source and commercial, are available to assist red teams in conducting effective reconnaissance. This chapter explores some of the most effective tools for reconnaissance, categorizing them based on their functions, and discussing their features, advantages, and best practices for use.

1. OSINT Tools

Open Source Intelligence (OSINT) tools are essential for gathering publicly available information about a target. These tools can extract data from various online sources, including websites, social media platforms, and public records.

Maltego

- **Overview**: Maltego is a powerful OSINT tool that specializes in visualizing relationships between different entities, such as people, domains, and organizations.
- **Features**: It provides a graphical interface that allows users to create interactive graphs showing connections between various data points, enabling red teams to **uncover** hidden relationships.
- Advantages: The ability to visualize complex relationships makes it easier to understand the target's network and identify potential attack vectors.
- **Best Practices**: Use Maltego to generate a comprehensive map of the target's infrastructure, and continually update the graph as new information is gathered.

Recon-ng

- **Overview**: Recon-ng is a web reconnaissance framework that provides a modular approach to collecting OSINT.
- **Features**: It offers various modules for tasks such as domain reconnaissance, social media analysis, and geographic data gathering.

- **Advantages**: Its modular design allows red teams to customize their reconnaissance efforts based on specific objectives.
- **Best Practices**: Familiarize yourself with the available modules and integrate them into a cohesive reconnaissance plan, documenting findings for later reference.

TheHarvester

- **Overview**: TheHarvester is an OSINT tool focused on collecting email addresses and subdomain names from public sources.
- **Features**: It scrapes information from search engines and social media platforms, allowing red teams to identify potential targets within an organization.
- **Advantages**: TheHarvester provides a quick way to gather contact information that can be useful for social engineering attacks.
- **Best Practices**: Use TheHarvester in conjunction with other OSINT tools to build a comprehensive profile of the target.

2. Network Scanning Tools

Network scanning tools are essential for identifying active devices, open ports, and services running on target systems. These tools help red teams map out the target's network infrastructure.

Nmap

- **Overview**: Nmap (Network Mapper) is a widely used open-source network scanning tool.
- **Features**: It offers a range of scanning options, including host discovery, port scanning, service identification, and operating system detection.
- **Advantages**: Nmap provides detailed information about the target's network and helps identify potential vulnerabilities that can be exploited.
- **Best Practices**: Perform regular scans and keep track of changes in the target's network to identify new services or potential vulnerabilities.

Masscan

- **Overview**: Masscan is a fast network scanner capable of scanning the entire internet in a short amount of time.
- **Features**: It uses asynchronous transmission to achieve high-speed scanning and can quickly identify open ports across large networks.

- **Advantages**: Its speed makes it particularly useful for conducting large-scale reconnaissance on multiple targets simultaneously.
- **Best Practices**: Use Masscan in conjunction with Nmap for a comprehensive analysis, using Masscan to identify open ports and Nmap for detailed service enumeration.

3. Vulnerability Scanning Tools

Vulnerability scanning tools help identify known vulnerabilities in systems and applications, providing red teams with valuable insights into potential weaknesses to exploit.

Nessus

- **Overview**: Nessus is a widely recognized vulnerability scanner that identifies security vulnerabilities in various systems and applications.
- **Features**: It provides a comprehensive list of vulnerabilities, including detailed descriptions, severity ratings, and remediation steps.
- **Advantages**: Nessus allows red teams to quickly assess the security posture of a target, highlighting areas that require immediate attention.
- **Best Practices**: Regularly update the vulnerability database to ensure that scans reflect the latest vulnerabilities, and prioritize remediation based on the severity of identified issues.

OpenVAS

- **Overview**: OpenVAS (Open Vulnerability Assessment System) is an open-source vulnerability scanner that provides similar functionality to Nessus.
- **Features**: It offers a comprehensive suite of tools for vulnerability scanning, management, and reporting.
- **Advantages**: Being open-source, OpenVAS provides a cost-effective alternative to commercial vulnerability scanners while still delivering robust capabilities.
- **Best Practices**: Use OpenVAS to complement Nessus, leveraging both tools for a thorough vulnerability assessment and ensuring that scanning schedules are well-coordinated.

4. Social Engineering Tools

Social engineering tools enable red teams to simulate human-based attacks and gather information through deception.

Social-Engineer Toolkit (SET)

- **Overview**: SET is an open-source tool designed to facilitate social engineering attacks.
- **Features**: It includes various features for phishing attacks, credential harvesting, and creating malicious payloads.
- **Advantages**: SET simplifies the process of creating convincing social engineering campaigns and allows red teams to test the human element of security.
- **Best Practices**: Use SET responsibly and with the consent of the target organization to avoid potential legal repercussions.

Ghostwriter

- **Overview**: Ghostwriter is a social engineering tool that allows users to create fake personas and engage in conversation on social media platforms.
- **Features**: It provides a platform for crafting realistic profiles and initiating conversations to gather information.
- **Advantages**: Ghostwriter can help red teams gather intelligence about employees and their behaviors without raising suspicion.
- **Best Practices**: Ensure that social engineering efforts are conducted ethically, and use the information gathered to inform subsequent testing phases.

5. Documentation and Analysis Tools

Effective reconnaissance requires proper documentation and analysis of gathered intelligence. The following tools assist in organizing and analyzing data.

Dradis

- **Overview**: Dradis is a collaboration and reporting tool that helps red teams manage their findings and streamline the reporting process.
- **Features**: It allows teams to document vulnerabilities, attack paths, and evidence in a centralized platform.
- **Advantages**: Dradis facilitates collaboration among team members, ensuring that findings are effectively communicated and organized.
- **Best Practices**: Use Dradis to create standardized reports that can be easily shared with stakeholders, ensuring consistent communication of findings.

Jira

- **Overview**: Jira is a project management tool that can be adapted for tracking vulnerabilities and managing remediation efforts.
- **Features**: It allows teams to create tickets for identified vulnerabilities, assign responsibilities, and track progress on remediation efforts.
- **Advantages**: Using Jira helps ensure that identified issues are addressed in a timely manner, improving the overall security posture of the organization.
- **Best Practices**: Integrate Jira with other tools to streamline the workflow and maintain clear communication among team members.

Utilizing the right tools for effective reconnaissance is vital for the success of red team operations. Each tool serves a specific purpose, whether it's gathering OSINT, scanning networks, identifying vulnerabilities, conducting social engineering, or documenting findings. By leveraging a combination of these tools and employing best practices, red teams can gather comprehensive intelligence about their targets, enabling them to develop effective attack strategies and enhance overall cybersecurity efforts. As the cyber threat landscape continues to evolve, staying updated on new tools and methodologies will be essential for maintaining an effective reconnaissance capability.

Chapter 7: Exploitation Techniques

In this chapter, we dive into the core of red teaming: exploitation techniques. This phase is where the groundwork laid during reconnaissance translates into action as red team members attempt to gain unauthorized access to systems and sensitive data. We will begin by discussing the process of vulnerability discovery and analysis, highlighting various methodologies for identifying weaknesses in applications, networks, and systems. Next, we will cover a range of common exploitation techniques, including SQL injection, cross-site scripting (XSS), and buffer overflows, providing practical examples of how these methods can be employed in real-world scenarios. Additionally, this chapter will introduce various tools and scripts that can streamline the exploitation process, allowing red team members to execute their strategies efficiently and effectively. By the end of this chapter, readers will have a thorough understanding of how to exploit vulnerabilities, equipped with both the theoretical knowledge and practical skills necessary to simulate real-world attacks and assess the security posture of their organizations comprehensively.

7.1 Vulnerability Discovery and Analysis

Vulnerability discovery and analysis are critical components of red team operations, playing a significant role in identifying weaknesses within an organization's systems, applications, and networks. This phase focuses on uncovering security flaws that could be exploited by malicious actors and providing insights into the potential impact of these vulnerabilities. This chapter delves into the various methods used for vulnerability discovery, the analysis of identified vulnerabilities, and best practices for effective management and remediation.

Understanding Vulnerabilities

Definition of Vulnerability:

A vulnerability is a weakness in a system, application, or network that can be exploited by an attacker to gain unauthorized access, disrupt operations, or cause damage. Vulnerabilities can arise from various factors, including software bugs, misconfigurations, and outdated technologies.

Types of Vulnerabilities:

- **Software Vulnerabilities**: Flaws in software code, such as buffer overflows, SQL injection, and cross-site scripting (XSS), can lead to unauthorized access or data exposure.
- **Configuration Vulnerabilities**: Misconfigurations in systems, firewalls, or network devices can create security gaps that attackers can exploit.
- **Human Vulnerabilities**: Weaknesses in human behavior, such as poor password practices or susceptibility to social engineering attacks, can lead to security breaches.
- **Protocol Vulnerabilities**: Flaws in network protocols can be exploited to intercept or manipulate data transmission.

Methods for Vulnerability Discovery

Automated Scanning:

Overview: Automated vulnerability scanners are tools that systematically assess systems and applications for known vulnerabilities. These tools can quickly scan large networks, identify security flaws, and generate detailed reports.

Examples:

- **Nessus**: A widely used vulnerability scanner that identifies vulnerabilities, misconfigurations, and compliance issues in various systems.
- **OpenVAS**: An open-source alternative to Nessus, providing robust vulnerability scanning capabilities.
- **Advantages**: Automated scanning enables rapid identification of known vulnerabilities and reduces the time required for manual assessments.

Manual Testing:

Overview: Manual vulnerability testing involves skilled security professionals systematically examining systems and applications for potential vulnerabilities. This approach allows for a deeper understanding of the target environment and the identification of complex vulnerabilities that automated tools may miss.

Techniques:

- **Static Analysis**: Reviewing source code or binaries without executing the program to identify potential vulnerabilities.

- **Dynamic Analysis**: Analyzing the behavior of an application during runtime to detect vulnerabilities in real time.
- **Advantages**: Manual testing provides a more thorough assessment and can uncover vulnerabilities that automated tools may overlook.

Fuzz Testing:

- **Overview**: Fuzz testing involves sending random or malformed data inputs to applications to trigger unexpected behavior and identify vulnerabilities.
- **Advantages**: This method can expose vulnerabilities related to input validation, buffer overflows, and error handling, which may not be detected through standard scanning techniques.

Penetration Testing:

- **Overview**: Penetration testing simulates real-world attacks on systems and applications to identify vulnerabilities that could be exploited by malicious actors. Red teams utilize various techniques, including social engineering, network attacks, and application exploits, to gain unauthorized access and assess security controls.
- **Advantages**: Penetration testing provides a realistic assessment of the organization's security posture and helps identify vulnerabilities in the context of actual attack scenarios.

Threat Intelligence:

Overview: Gathering threat intelligence from various sources, such as security advisories, vulnerability databases, and industry reports, can provide insights into emerging vulnerabilities and threats. Understanding the threat landscape helps organizations prioritize vulnerabilities based on their potential impact.

Sources:

- **National Vulnerability Database (NVD):** A comprehensive repository of known vulnerabilities.
- **CVE (Common Vulnerabilities and Exposures):** A standardized list of publicly known cybersecurity vulnerabilities.
- **Advantages**: By staying informed about the latest vulnerabilities, organizations can proactively address security gaps before they are exploited.

Analyzing Identified Vulnerabilities

Risk Assessment:

Overview: Once vulnerabilities are discovered, it is essential to assess the risk they pose to the organization. This involves evaluating the potential impact of each vulnerability, the likelihood of exploitation, and the overall risk to the organization's assets.

Factors to Consider:

- **Severity**: Classify vulnerabilities based on their severity level (e.g., critical, high, medium, low) using standardized frameworks such as CVSS (Common Vulnerability Scoring System).
- **Asset Value**: Consider the value of the affected asset to the organization and the potential consequences of a successful attack.
- **Threat Landscape**: Evaluate the current threat landscape to determine the likelihood of exploitation by attackers.

Exploitation Potential:

Overview: Understanding the potential for exploitation is crucial for prioritizing vulnerabilities for remediation. This involves evaluating the technical feasibility of exploiting each vulnerability, as well as any mitigating factors that may reduce the likelihood of an attack.

Techniques:

- **Exploit Development**: In some cases, red teams may develop proof-of-concept exploits to demonstrate the feasibility of an attack.
- **Testing for Exploitability**: Conducting controlled tests to determine whether a vulnerability can be successfully exploited in a specific environment.

Impact Analysis:

- **Overview**: Analyzing the potential impact of a successful exploit helps organizations understand the consequences of vulnerabilities. This includes considering factors such as data loss, service disruption, reputational damage, and legal implications.

- **Outcome**: This analysis provides valuable insights for decision-making regarding which vulnerabilities to prioritize for remediation and the necessary resources to allocate.

Prioritization and Remediation Planning:

Overview: After assessing the risks and potential impacts, red teams should prioritize vulnerabilities for remediation based on their severity, exploitability, and business context. This prioritization helps organizations allocate resources effectively and address the most critical vulnerabilities first.

Remediation Strategies:

- **Patch Management**: Apply patches and updates to address vulnerabilities in software and systems.
- **Configuration Changes**: Adjust configurations to mitigate risks associated with misconfigurations.
- **Compensating Controls**: Implement additional security controls to reduce the risk of exploitation, such as network segmentation or intrusion detection systems.

Best Practices for Vulnerability Discovery and Analysis

Regular Scanning and Assessments:

Conduct regular vulnerability scans and assessments to identify new vulnerabilities as they arise. Regular assessments help organizations stay ahead of emerging threats and ensure that security controls remain effective.

Integrate into Development Lifecycle:

Incorporate vulnerability discovery and analysis into the software development lifecycle (SDLC). By conducting security assessments during the development phase, organizations can identify and address vulnerabilities before applications are deployed.

Maintain an Inventory of Assets:

Keep an up-to-date inventory of all assets, including hardware, software, and cloud services. An accurate inventory ensures that all components are assessed for vulnerabilities and helps prioritize remediation efforts.

Document Findings:

Document all discovered vulnerabilities, analysis results, and remediation efforts. This documentation serves as a valuable resource for future assessments and helps track progress in addressing security gaps.

Stay Informed About Threats:

Continuously monitor threat intelligence sources and industry reports to stay informed about emerging vulnerabilities and attacks. Understanding the threat landscape enables organizations to prioritize their vulnerability management efforts effectively.

Train and Educate Teams:

Ensure that security teams are trained on the latest vulnerability discovery techniques and analysis methods. Regular training helps keep teams updated on best practices and emerging threats.

Vulnerability discovery and analysis are vital components of red team operations, enabling organizations to identify and address weaknesses in their systems, applications, and networks. By employing a combination of automated scanning, manual testing, fuzz testing, penetration testing, and threat intelligence, red teams can uncover vulnerabilities that pose risks to organizational assets. Following a structured approach to analyzing identified vulnerabilities ensures that organizations can prioritize remediation efforts effectively and strengthen their overall security posture. As the cyber threat landscape continues to evolve, ongoing vulnerability discovery and analysis will remain essential for proactive risk management and maintaining robust cybersecurity defenses.

7.2 Common Exploitation Techniques

In the realm of cybersecurity, exploitation techniques are the methods by which attackers leverage identified vulnerabilities to gain unauthorized access, escalate privileges, or cause harm to a target system or network. Understanding these techniques is crucial for red teams, as it allows them to simulate real-world attacks and effectively test an organization's defenses. This chapter will explore several common exploitation techniques, their mechanics, and how they can be used in a red team context.

1. Buffer Overflow Exploits

Overview: A buffer overflow occurs when a program writes more data to a buffer than it can hold, leading to data corruption, crashes, or arbitrary code execution. This type of vulnerability can be exploited to gain control of a target system.

Mechanics:

Attack Vector: An attacker provides more data than a buffer can accommodate, overwriting adjacent memory locations. This can allow an attacker to overwrite the return address of a function, redirecting execution to malicious code.

Exploitation Steps:

- Identify a vulnerable program that accepts user input.
- Craft a payload that exceeds the buffer size, including shellcode.
- Send the payload to the application, causing it to execute the attacker's code.

Example: In a classic buffer overflow exploit, an attacker might target a C program that does not properly validate input. By sending a crafted input string that exceeds the buffer size, the attacker can redirect program execution to their shellcode.

Mitigations:

- Employ stack canaries to detect buffer overflows.
- Use Address Space Layout Randomization (ASLR) to randomize memory addresses, making it difficult for attackers to predict where to jump.
- Implement data execution prevention (DEP) to mark memory regions as non-executable.

2. SQL Injection

Overview: SQL injection is a web application vulnerability that allows attackers to manipulate SQL queries by injecting malicious SQL code through input fields. This technique can lead to unauthorized data access, modification, or even complete database control.

Mechanics:

Attack Vector: An attacker inputs specially crafted SQL statements into input fields that are directly used in SQL queries without proper sanitization.

Exploitation Steps:

- Identify an input field vulnerable to SQL injection (e.g., login forms, search bars).
- Craft an SQL payload that alters the intended query, such as bypassing authentication or extracting sensitive data.
- Submit the crafted input to execute the malicious SQL command.

Example: An attacker may input ' OR '1'='1' -- into a login form. This input alters the SQL query to always return true, allowing the attacker to log in without valid credentials.

Mitigations:

- Use parameterized queries or prepared statements to safely handle user input.
- Implement input validation and output encoding to prevent injection.
- Employ web application firewalls (WAFs) to detect and block SQL injection attempts.

3. Cross-Site Scripting (XSS)

Overview: Cross-Site Scripting (XSS) allows attackers to inject malicious scripts into web pages viewed by users. This technique can lead to session hijacking, data theft, and malicious actions performed on behalf of the user.

Mechanics:

Attack Vector: An attacker injects a script into a web application that does not properly sanitize user input before rendering it on a web page.

Exploitation Steps:

- Identify a vulnerable input field where user input is reflected in the output.
- Craft a malicious JavaScript payload.
- Trigger the script by convincing users to click on a malicious link or by embedding the script in a trusted web page.

Example: An attacker might inject a script that steals cookies and sends them to their server, effectively hijacking the user's session.

Mitigations:

- Implement Content Security Policy (CSP) to restrict the execution of scripts.
- Sanitize and encode user inputs and outputs.
- Regularly review web application code for potential XSS vulnerabilities.

4. Command Injection

Overview: Command injection vulnerabilities occur when an attacker can execute arbitrary commands on a host operating system through a vulnerable application. This can allow attackers to take control of the system or access sensitive data.

Mechanics:

Attack Vector: An attacker sends specially crafted input to a vulnerable application that constructs system commands without proper validation.

Exploitation Steps:

- Identify an application that allows for shell command execution.
- Craft an input that includes additional commands (e.g., using a semicolon to terminate the original command).
- Submit the input, leading to execution of the attacker's command.

Example: If a web application allows users to ping an IP address through an input field, an attacker could input 127.0.0.1; ls to execute the ls command on the server.

Mitigations:

- Validate and sanitize all user inputs.
- Use whitelisting to restrict acceptable commands and inputs.
- Implement least privilege principles to limit the permissions of applications.

5. Privilege Escalation

Overview: Privilege escalation exploits vulnerabilities to gain higher access rights than initially granted. This technique allows attackers to execute actions that would normally require elevated permissions.

Mechanics:

Types of Escalation:

- **Vertical Escalation**: Gaining higher privileges, such as a user gaining administrative rights.
- **Horizontal Escalation**: Accessing resources or data of another user with the same privilege level.

Exploitation Steps:

- Identify vulnerabilities in the system that allow privilege escalation, such as misconfigured services or unpatched software.
- Leverage these vulnerabilities to execute commands or gain access to restricted areas.

Example: An attacker might exploit a known vulnerability in an outdated service running with elevated privileges to gain root access to the system.

Mitigations:

- Regularly update and patch systems and applications to address known vulnerabilities.
- Employ strict access controls and regularly review user privileges.
- Implement security monitoring to detect unusual activities that may indicate privilege escalation attempts.

6. Denial of Service (DoS) and Distributed Denial of Service (DDoS)

Overview: DoS and DDoS attacks aim to overwhelm a target system, network, or service, rendering it unavailable to legitimate users. These attacks can disrupt business operations and cause significant financial losses.

Mechanics:

- **DoS Attacks**: An attacker uses a single machine to flood a target with excessive requests or traffic, exhausting system resources.
- **DDoS Attacks**: Multiple compromised machines (often part of a botnet) are used to launch a coordinated attack, increasing the volume and complexity of the attack.

Exploitation Steps:

- Identify a target service or application.
- Use tools or scripts to send a high volume of traffic to the target.
- Monitor the target's response and effectiveness of the attack.

Example: An attacker could use a DDoS tool to launch a massive volume of traffic against an e-commerce site, rendering it inaccessible during peak shopping hours.

Mitigations:

- Implement rate limiting to control the number of requests a user can make.
- Use content delivery networks (CDNs) to absorb and mitigate traffic spikes.
- Deploy DDoS protection services that can detect and respond to attack patterns.

7. Credential Stuffing

Overview: Credential stuffing is an automated attack method where attackers use stolen username and password combinations to gain unauthorized access to user accounts across multiple services.

Mechanics:

Attack Vector: Attackers leverage credential databases from previous breaches to attempt logins on various websites.

Exploitation Steps:

- Acquire a list of compromised credentials from a data breach.
- Use automated tools to test these credentials across multiple platforms.
- Gain unauthorized access to accounts, often leading to further exploitation.

Example: An attacker uses credentials obtained from a data breach of one service to gain access to users' accounts on unrelated platforms.

Mitigations:

- Implement multi-factor authentication (MFA) to add an additional layer of security.

- Encourage users to use unique passwords for different services.
- Monitor login attempts for unusual patterns that may indicate credential stuffing.

Understanding common exploitation techniques is vital for red teams and organizations aiming to strengthen their cybersecurity posture. By familiarizing themselves with these techniques, red teams can effectively simulate attacks, identify vulnerabilities, and provide valuable insights for remediation efforts. This proactive approach enables organizations to mitigate risks, enhance their defenses, and ultimately safeguard their assets against real-world cyber threats. Ongoing training, threat intelligence, and awareness of evolving exploitation techniques will further empower red teams to stay ahead of attackers and ensure a robust security framework.

7.3 Tools and Scripts for Exploitation

In the field of cybersecurity, particularly in red teaming, a variety of tools and scripts are employed to execute exploitation techniques. These tools enable security professionals to automate tasks, streamline processes, and effectively simulate real-world attack scenarios. This chapter will discuss some of the most widely used tools and scripts in exploitation, their functionalities, and their application in red team operations.

1. Metasploit Framework

Overview: The Metasploit Framework is one of the most popular and powerful penetration testing tools available. It provides a comprehensive platform for developing, testing, and executing exploits against target systems.

Key Features:

- **Exploit Modules**: Metasploit comes with a vast library of pre-built exploits targeting various vulnerabilities across multiple platforms.
- **Payloads**: Users can choose from numerous payloads that determine the actions taken once an exploit is successful, such as opening a reverse shell or executing a command.
- **Post-Exploitation Modules**: After gaining access, red teamers can use post-exploitation modules to gather information, escalate privileges, and maintain persistence.
- **Community Contributions**: Metasploit is an open-source project, and the community continually contributes new modules and updates.

Usage:

To use Metasploit, red teamers typically launch the Metasploit console and select an exploit module to target a specific vulnerability. They configure the target parameters and payload before executing the exploit.

Example: A red teamer can use Metasploit to exploit a vulnerable web application by selecting an appropriate SQL injection exploit, configuring the payload to retrieve database credentials, and executing the attack.

2. Nmap

Overview: Nmap (Network Mapper) is a versatile open-source tool primarily used for network discovery and security auditing. While not strictly an exploitation tool, it plays a crucial role in the reconnaissance phase and can assist in identifying exploitable services.

Key Features:

- **Port Scanning**: Nmap can quickly scan a range of IP addresses to discover open ports and services running on the target system.
- **Service Version Detection**: Nmap can identify the version of services running, helping to determine known vulnerabilities associated with those versions.
- **Scripting Engine**: Nmap includes a powerful scripting engine (NSE) that allows users to write and execute scripts for advanced scanning and exploitation tasks.

Usage:

Red teamers often use Nmap to gather initial information about a target, identifying which services are running and their associated vulnerabilities. The scripting engine can also be used to automate vulnerability checks.

Example: A red teamer might use Nmap to scan a target for open ports and then leverage NSE scripts to check for vulnerabilities associated with the identified services.

3. Burp Suite

Overview: Burp Suite is an integrated platform for web application security testing. It is widely used for manual and automated testing of web applications, including the exploitation of vulnerabilities like SQL injection and XSS.

Key Features:

- **Intercepting Proxy**: Burp Suite allows users to intercept and modify HTTP requests and responses, enabling deep inspection of web application traffic.
- **Scanner**: The automated scanner can identify common web vulnerabilities, including SQL injection, XSS, and CSRF (Cross-Site Request Forgery).
- **Intruder**: The Intruder tool can be used to perform automated attacks, such as brute-forcing credentials or fuzzing input fields.
- **Repeater**: The Repeater allows users to manually modify and resend requests to test for vulnerabilities.

Usage:

Red teamers use Burp Suite to analyze web application traffic, identify vulnerabilities, and exploit them using various tools within the suite.

Example: A red teamer could use Burp Suite to intercept a request to a login form, modify the parameters to attempt SQL injection, and observe the application's response to identify potential vulnerabilities.

4. Cobalt Strike

Overview: Cobalt Strike is a commercial penetration testing tool that provides advanced capabilities for red teaming, including exploitation, post-exploitation, and command-and-control (C2) functionalities.

Key Features:

- **Beacon Payload**: Cobalt Strike's Beacon payload allows for command and control over compromised systems, enabling attackers to execute commands and move laterally within a network.
- **Social Engineering Tools**: Cobalt Strike includes features for phishing attacks, allowing red teamers to simulate realistic attacks.
- **Post-Exploitation Features**: The tool provides extensive post-exploitation capabilities, including credential harvesting, keystroke logging, and remote command execution.

Usage:

Red teamers often use Cobalt Strike to simulate sophisticated attack scenarios, leveraging its capabilities for command and control, lateral movement, and persistence.

Example: After exploiting a vulnerable application, a red teamer could use Cobalt Strike's Beacon to maintain access to the compromised system and execute commands for further exploration.

5. PowerShell Empire

Overview: PowerShell Empire is a post-exploitation framework that allows attackers to control Windows systems using PowerShell. It provides a variety of modules for exploitation and lateral movement.

Key Features:

- **Agent Management**: PowerShell Empire allows users to manage agents (compromised systems) and execute commands on them remotely.
- **Post-Exploitation Modules**: The framework includes numerous modules for privilege escalation, credential dumping, and lateral movement.
- **Bypass Defenses**: PowerShell Empire can help bypass security measures like antivirus and endpoint detection systems through its use of PowerShell scripts.

Usage:

Red teamers can deploy PowerShell Empire to maintain access to Windows systems and execute commands for further exploitation and data exfiltration.

Example: After compromising a Windows machine, a red teamer might use PowerShell Empire to dump credentials from the Windows Credential Manager and move laterally to other systems.

6. SQLMap

Overview: SQLMap is an open-source tool specifically designed for detecting and exploiting SQL injection vulnerabilities in web applications. It automates the process of testing and exploiting SQL injection.

Key Features:

- **Automated Detection**: SQLMap can automatically detect SQL injection vulnerabilities and identify the type of database in use.
- **Data Extraction**: The tool can extract data from databases, including user credentials and sensitive information.
- **Database Management**: SQLMap allows users to perform various database management operations, such as table and column enumeration.

Usage:

Red teamers often use SQLMap to quickly identify and exploit SQL injection vulnerabilities, automating the extraction of sensitive data from compromised databases.

Example: A red teamer might use SQLMap to target a vulnerable web application and extract user data from the underlying database by executing automated SQL injection attacks.

7. Exploit-DB

Overview: Exploit Database (Exploit-DB) is an online repository of public exploits and corresponding vulnerable software. It serves as a valuable resource for security professionals seeking to understand vulnerabilities and their exploitation.

Key Features:

- **Searchable Database**: Users can search for exploits based on software name, platform, or type of vulnerability.
- **Documentation**: Each exploit entry includes documentation, potential impact, and examples of how to execute the exploit.
- **Community Contributions**: The database is regularly updated with new exploits submitted by the security community.

Usage:

Red teamers can leverage Exploit-DB to find existing exploits for vulnerabilities discovered during assessments, enabling them to simulate real-world attacks.

Example: A red teamer might search Exploit-DB for known exploits related to a specific version of a web application to gain insights into potential attack vectors.

8. Custom Scripts

Overview: In addition to established tools, red teamers often create custom scripts to tailor their exploitation techniques to specific environments or scenarios.

Key Features:

- **Flexibility**: Custom scripts can be designed to target unique vulnerabilities or adapt existing exploitation techniques to fit specific needs.
- **Automation**: Scripts can automate repetitive tasks, streamline workflows, and reduce the time required for manual exploitation.

Usage:

Red teamers use languages like Python, Ruby, and Bash to develop scripts that perform specific tasks, such as brute-forcing passwords, automating payload delivery, or executing reconnaissance tasks.

Example: A red teamer might write a Python script that automates the process of testing a list of usernames and passwords against a vulnerable login page, quickly identifying valid credentials.

The landscape of exploitation tools and scripts is diverse, offering red teamers a wide array of options for simulating attacks and testing security defenses. From powerful frameworks like Metasploit and Cobalt Strike to specialized tools like SQLMap and Burp Suite, these resources are essential for effectively identifying and exploiting vulnerabilities. Additionally, custom scripts can enhance flexibility and enable tailored approaches to specific scenarios. By leveraging these tools and maintaining up-to-date knowledge of their capabilities, red teams can effectively assess and improve an organization's security posture, ultimately helping to mitigate risks and strengthen defenses against real-world cyber threats.

Chapter 8: Post-Exploitation Strategies

In this chapter, we explore the critical phase of post-exploitation, where the focus shifts from gaining access to maintaining control and extracting valuable information. This stage is essential for understanding the full impact of a successful red team engagement and simulating the actions of real-world attackers. We will begin by discussing techniques for maintaining access and persistence within a compromised environment, examining methods such as establishing backdoors and exploiting legitimate administrative tools. Next, we will delve into data exfiltration strategies, detailing how attackers can stealthily extract sensitive information without detection, including the use of covert channels and encryption techniques. Additionally, we will cover the importance of clearing tracks and erasing traces of the attack to avoid detection, highlighting techniques for log manipulation and evidence removal. By the end of this chapter, readers will gain a comprehensive understanding of post-exploitation strategies, empowering them to assess the potential long-term impact of vulnerabilities and to enhance their organization's defensive measures against sophisticated attacks.

8.1 Maintaining Access and Persistence

Maintaining access and persistence are critical components of a successful red team operation. After successfully exploiting a target system, red teamers aim to establish a foothold within the environment, allowing them to conduct further exploration and potentially escalate privileges or access sensitive data. This chapter will explore various techniques for maintaining access, methods for ensuring persistence, and best practices for managing these activities during red team engagements.

Understanding Access and Persistence

Access refers to the ability of an attacker to log into a compromised system and interact with its resources. Persistence, on the other hand, refers to the methods used by attackers to maintain access to a system even after the initial exploitation is detected or the system is rebooted. Understanding how to effectively achieve both access and persistence is crucial for red teamers as they emulate the tactics used by real-world attackers.

Techniques for Maintaining Access

Backdoors

- **Definition**: A backdoor is a hidden method of bypassing normal authentication or security controls in a system, providing an attacker with a way to access the system later without needing to exploit a vulnerability again.
- **Implementation**: Red teamers can create a backdoor by modifying existing applications, installing custom software, or using scripting languages like PowerShell or Python to deploy malicious code that listens for incoming connections.
- **Example**: An attacker might install a remote access trojan (RAT) on a compromised machine that opens a port, allowing them to connect at will.

Credential Harvesting

Definition: Credential harvesting involves extracting user credentials from a compromised system, which can then be used to access other systems or services within the target environment.

Techniques:

- **Keylogging**: Installing keyloggers to capture user input, particularly passwords.
- **Credential Dumping**: Using tools like Mimikatz to extract stored passwords from memory or the Windows Security Account Manager (SAM).
- **Example**: After gaining access to a Windows system, a red teamer might run Mimikatz to dump user credentials from memory, allowing them to move laterally within the network.

Web Shells

- **Definition**: A web shell is a malicious script that can be uploaded to a web server, allowing an attacker to execute commands remotely through a web interface.
- **Implementation**: Red teamers can exploit a vulnerable web application to upload a web shell, enabling them to run commands on the server as if they were the legitimate user.
- **Example**: An attacker might exploit a file upload vulnerability in a web application to upload a PHP shell, which they can then access via a web browser to execute arbitrary commands.

Techniques for Ensuring Persistence

Scheduled Tasks and Cron Jobs

Definition: Scheduled tasks (Windows) and cron jobs (Linux) are automated tasks that run at specified intervals. Attackers can use these features to create tasks that re-establish access after a system reboot or a user logs out.

Implementation:

- **Windows**: A red teamer can create a scheduled task that runs a malicious script or binary upon system startup or user login.
- **Linux**: An attacker can create a cron job that executes a command or script regularly.
- **Example**: An attacker might create a Windows scheduled task that runs a reverse shell every time the system boots, ensuring continued access.

Service Creation

- **Definition**: Attackers can create new services on a compromised system that automatically execute malicious code whenever the system starts.
- **Implementation**: Using administrative privileges, red teamers can create a new service using Windows Service Control Manager (SCM) or Linux service management tools (like systemd).
- **Example**: An attacker might create a Windows service that runs a malicious executable every time the system is powered on or restarted.

Registry Modifications

- **Definition**: Modifying the Windows registry allows attackers to create persistence mechanisms by altering the registry keys that dictate which programs run at startup.
- **Implementation**: Red teamers can add entries to the Run or RunOnce keys, which execute specified programs upon user login or system startup.
- **Example**: An attacker might add their malicious executable to the HKEY_CURRENT_USER\Software\Microsoft\Windows\CurrentVersion\Run registry key to ensure it runs every time a user logs in.

Browser Extensions

- **Definition**: Attackers can exploit browser vulnerabilities to install malicious extensions that maintain persistence by running whenever the browser is open.
- **Implementation**: By compromising a user's account or exploiting vulnerabilities, red teamers can deploy malicious extensions that allow for ongoing control or data exfiltration.
- **Example**: An attacker might create a malicious browser extension that captures and forwards user data to an external server whenever the browser is in use.

Best Practices for Maintaining Access and Persistence

Operational Security (OpSec): Maintaining proper operational security is essential for red teamers to avoid detection during their operations. This includes careful planning and execution of access and persistence techniques to minimize footprints.

Documentation: Red teamers should meticulously document all actions taken to maintain access and establish persistence. This documentation can provide valuable insights during the debriefing and reporting phases of the engagement.

Adapting to the Environment: Each environment is unique, and red teamers must adapt their techniques based on the specific security controls and configurations in place. Understanding the target environment is crucial for selecting the most effective methods.

Testing Detection Capabilities: Red teams should also assess the organization's ability to detect unauthorized access and persistence mechanisms. This involves deliberately triggering alerts and monitoring responses to improve incident response strategies.

Collaboration with Blue Teams: In some engagements, red teams may work closely with blue teams (defensive security teams) to enhance overall security posture. This collaboration can provide insights into real-world attack techniques and improve defensive measures.

Maintaining access and ensuring persistence are vital for red team operations, allowing security professionals to simulate real-world attacks and assess the effectiveness of an organization's defenses. By employing various techniques such as backdoors, credential harvesting, web shells, scheduled tasks, service creation, registry modifications, and browser extensions, red teamers can establish footholds within target environments. Best practices, including operational security and thorough documentation, help maintain stealth and effectiveness during engagements. Ultimately, understanding and implementing these concepts allows red teams to provide valuable insights to organizations, helping them strengthen their cybersecurity posture and respond to real-world threats effectively.

8.2 Data Exfiltration Techniques

Data exfiltration is a critical phase in a cyberattack, particularly for red teams simulating real-world adversarial tactics. It involves the unauthorized transfer of sensitive information from a target environment to an external location controlled by an attacker. This chapter explores various data exfiltration techniques, highlighting their methods, tools, and best practices to emulate sophisticated attacks during red team engagements.

Understanding Data Exfiltration

Data exfiltration refers to the process by which attackers acquire and transfer data from a target system or network without authorization. The goal is often to obtain sensitive information such as intellectual property, personal identifiable information (PII), financial records, or proprietary data. Understanding the methods of data exfiltration allows red teams to demonstrate the potential risks to organizations and identify weaknesses in their security measures.

Techniques for Data Exfiltration

Network Protocols

Overview: Attackers often leverage existing network protocols to exfiltrate data, using techniques that blend in with normal network traffic to avoid detection.

Common Protocols:

- **HTTP/HTTPS**: Using standard web traffic to send data to an external server.
- **FTP/SFTP**: Utilizing file transfer protocols to move files directly from the compromised environment to an attacker-controlled server.
- **DNS Tunneling**: Encoding data within DNS queries, allowing attackers to transfer data through DNS requests.
- **Example**: An attacker might use an HTTP POST request to send sensitive files from a compromised server to a remote server under their control, disguising the data as legitimate web traffic.

Cloud Storage Services

Overview: Many organizations use cloud storage solutions (e.g., Dropbox, Google Drive, OneDrive) for data storage and sharing. Attackers can exploit these services for exfiltration.

Methods:

- **Account Compromise**: Using stolen credentials to access legitimate accounts and transfer data to the attacker's cloud storage.
- **API Abuse**: Leveraging cloud storage APIs to programmatically upload files from a compromised system.
- **Example**: After gaining access to a corporate account, an attacker could upload sensitive documents to a personal Google Drive account, bypassing traditional security measures.

Physical Media

Overview: In certain scenarios, attackers may use physical media such as USB drives to exfiltrate data, especially in environments with strict network security controls.

Methods:

- **Manual Copying**: Physically accessing a system and manually copying data to a USB drive or external hard disk.
- **Automated Scripts**: Deploying scripts that automatically transfer sensitive files to attached USB drives when connected to a compromised machine.
- **Example**: An insider threat or an external attacker with physical access might copy sensitive financial records onto a USB drive before leaving the premises.

Email and Messaging Services

Overview: Attackers can utilize email and messaging platforms to exfiltrate data discreetly.

Methods:

- **Steganography**: Hiding data within images or documents and sending them via email, where the data is extracted upon receipt.

- **Phishing and Social Engineering**: Manipulating employees into sending sensitive data via email or messaging platforms under false pretenses.
- **Example**: An attacker could embed sensitive data within an image file and email it to their account, where they can extract the data later.

Command and Control (C2) Channels

Overview: Establishing a command and control channel allows attackers to maintain communication with compromised systems and transfer data.

Methods:

- **Reverse Shells**: Using reverse shells to send data back to the attacker's server as commands are executed.
- **Data Dumps**: Sending large quantities of data in batches through the C2 channel to minimize detection.
- **Example**: An attacker with a reverse shell on a compromised machine might periodically send chunks of sensitive data back to their server while maintaining control over the system.

Local Network Transfers

Overview: Attackers can exploit local network protocols to exfiltrate data to other systems on the same network.

Methods:

- **SMB (Server Message Block):** Using SMB shares to transfer files directly to a system controlled by the attacker.
- **RDP (Remote Desktop Protocol):** Gaining access to another system on the network and transferring data directly.
- **Example**: An attacker could use SMB to copy sensitive files from a compromised workstation to a rogue server within the same local network.

Data Compression and Encryption

Overview: To avoid detection during exfiltration, attackers may compress and encrypt data before transferring it.

Methods:

- **Zipping**: Compressing files into a ZIP archive to reduce their size and obfuscate contents.
- **Encryption**: Encrypting data before exfiltration to prevent detection by security systems analyzing data content.
- **Example**: An attacker may compress and encrypt sensitive documents, making it difficult for security systems to identify the data during transfer.

Best Practices for Red Team Data Exfiltration

Simulating Real-World Scenarios: When conducting data exfiltration during red team exercises, it's important to emulate real-world tactics and techniques that attackers might use, providing valuable insights into potential vulnerabilities.

Documenting Techniques: Red teamers should meticulously document all exfiltration methods used, including tools and techniques employed. This documentation is essential for later debriefings and for informing the target organization of specific vulnerabilities.

Testing Detection Mechanisms: Red teams should also assess the organization's ability to detect data exfiltration attempts. This could involve triggering alerts and monitoring responses, which helps in improving the overall security posture.

Adapting Techniques to the Environment: Each environment is unique, and red teamers should tailor their exfiltration techniques based on the specific security controls in place at the target organization.

Using Stealth Techniques: To emulate sophisticated attackers, red teams should focus on stealthy exfiltration techniques that blend in with normal traffic patterns, minimizing the chances of detection by security systems.

Data exfiltration is a crucial aspect of red team operations, simulating the tactics and techniques employed by real-world adversaries. By utilizing various methods, including network protocols, cloud services, physical media, email, C2 channels, and local network transfers, red teamers can effectively demonstrate the risks of unauthorized data transfer. Understanding these techniques and best practices enables organizations to bolster their defenses against potential data breaches, ultimately improving their overall cybersecurity posture.

8.3 Clearing Tracks and Evidence

Clearing tracks and evidence is a critical aspect of any cyber operation, especially for red teams emulating the tactics of sophisticated adversaries. After successfully conducting an attack or exfiltrating data, an attacker must take measures to erase their presence and obscure their activities, making it difficult for defenders to detect and respond to the breach. This chapter explores various techniques employed to clear tracks and evidence, the tools used, and best practices that red teams can adopt to effectively simulate these tactics.

Understanding Track Clearing

Track clearing refers to the actions taken to remove or obfuscate evidence of malicious activity within a system or network. This involves erasing logs, modifying timestamps, and employing various techniques to ensure that the attacker's actions remain undetected. For red teams, understanding how to clear tracks is vital not only for simulating real-world attacks but also for assessing the effectiveness of an organization's incident response and logging capabilities.

Techniques for Clearing Tracks and Evidence

Log Manipulation

Overview: Logs are critical for monitoring and analyzing system activities. Attackers often manipulate or delete logs to hide their actions from security personnel.

Methods:

- **Log Deletion**: Permanently removing logs from the system to erase any evidence of the attack.
- **Log Modification**: Altering log entries to change timestamps, source IP addresses, or other identifying information to mislead investigators.
- **Example**: An attacker might delete specific event log entries on a Windows system that indicate unauthorized access or suspicious activities.

Clearing Command History

Overview: Command history files record the commands executed in a terminal or command prompt. Clearing these files is essential for removing traces of malicious actions.

Methods:

- **Shell Commands**: Using built-in shell commands to delete history entries, such as history -c in bash or clearing PowerShell history.
- **Manual Deletion**: Locating and deleting history files directly from the file system.
- **Example**: An attacker using a Linux system might run history -c followed by rm ~/.bash_history to clear all traces of their activities in the terminal.

Timestamps Manipulation

Overview: Attackers may alter timestamps associated with files and logs to obscure the timeline of their actions.

Methods:

- **Using touch Command**: In Linux, the touch command can be used to change the timestamps of files, making it appear as though they were created or modified at a different time.
- **PowerShell Scripts**: In Windows, PowerShell can be used to modify file timestamps programmatically.
- **Example**: An attacker might modify the timestamps of a backdoor executable to match legitimate file activity, making it more difficult for forensic analysts to identify malicious files.

Clearing Temporary Files and Artifacts

Overview: Many tools and malware create temporary files or leave artifacts behind that can be used for forensic analysis. Clearing these files helps to eliminate traces of an attack.

Methods:

- **Temporary File Cleanup**: Deleting temporary files created by applications or the operating system that may contain evidence of malicious activity.
- **Application-Specific Data Removal**: Clearing caches, cookies, and logs from browsers or other applications used during the attack.
- **Example**: An attacker might clear the browser cache or delete temporary files from the system to remove any indicators of web-based attacks.

Using Anti-Forensics Tools

Overview: Anti-forensics tools are specifically designed to hinder forensic investigations by modifying or deleting evidence of malicious activities.

Methods:

- **Data Wiping Tools**: Using software that securely deletes files, ensuring they cannot be recovered by forensic tools.
- **Log Spoofing**: Utilizing tools that create fake log entries to mislead investigators.
- **Example**: An attacker might deploy a data wiping tool that uses multiple overwrite passes to ensure that deleted files cannot be recovered, thereby preventing forensic analysis.

Network Traffic Obfuscation

Overview: Attackers may attempt to obfuscate network traffic to hide their activities from monitoring tools.

Methods:

- **Encryption**: Using encrypted tunnels (e.g., VPNs or SSH) to hide data exfiltration traffic from network monitoring systems.
- **Protocol Spoofing**: Manipulating packet headers to disguise malicious traffic as legitimate communication.
- **Example**: An attacker could use an SSH tunnel to send exfiltrated data, making it appear as if normal encrypted traffic is being transmitted.

Using Virtual Environments

Overview: Virtual environments, such as virtual machines (VMs), can provide a layer of separation from the host system, allowing attackers to operate without leaving traces on the physical hardware.

Methods:

- **Temporary Virtual Machines**: Creating temporary VMs for conducting attacks and deleting them afterward to eliminate evidence.
- **Snapshots**: Taking snapshots of a VM before executing malicious activities and reverting to the snapshot afterward to clear tracks.

- **Example**: An attacker might deploy a VM to conduct reconnaissance and exploit a target system, then delete the VM after the operation, erasing all traces of their activities.

Best Practices for Red Teams

Understand Organizational Logging: Red teams should have a deep understanding of the target organization's logging practices and capabilities. This knowledge helps them identify potential areas to manipulate or clear tracks effectively.

Document Techniques Used: While it may seem counterintuitive, documenting the methods used to clear tracks is essential. This information can be invaluable during debriefing sessions, allowing organizations to understand and improve their detection capabilities.

Simulate Real-World Scenarios: When conducting exercises, red teams should aim to replicate the techniques used by real-world adversaries. This includes using a combination of techniques tailored to the specific environment being tested.

Evaluate Detection Mechanisms: Red teams should evaluate how effective the organization's detection mechanisms are against the track-clearing techniques used. This evaluation will help inform security improvements and incident response planning.

Collaboration with Blue Teams: In certain engagements, red teams may work alongside blue teams to enhance overall security. This collaboration can provide insights into the effectiveness of detection methods and improve the organization's overall cybersecurity posture.

Clearing tracks and evidence is a vital aspect of red team operations, simulating the tactics used by real-world attackers to evade detection. By employing various techniques, including log manipulation, command history clearing, timestamp modification, and the use of anti-forensics tools, red teamers can effectively demonstrate the risks associated with malicious activity. Understanding and implementing these methods not only helps red teams mimic sophisticated attacks but also provides organizations with valuable insights to improve their security measures and response capabilities against real-world threats.

Chapter 9: Social Engineering Tactics

In this chapter, we delve into the often-overlooked but critically important realm of social engineering tactics, where psychological manipulation is employed to deceive individuals and gain unauthorized access to information or systems. We will begin by defining social engineering and discussing its significance in the broader context of red teaming, emphasizing how human factors can often be the weakest link in an organization's security posture. Next, we will explore various social engineering techniques, including pretexting, baiting, and tailgating, providing real-world examples to illustrate their effectiveness. The chapter will also cover the role of phishing simulations, detailing how red teams can assess an organization's susceptibility to these tactics and promote awareness among employees. Furthermore, we will discuss the importance of implementing effective training programs to enhance staff resilience against social engineering attacks. By the conclusion of this chapter, readers will have a comprehensive understanding of social engineering tactics and be equipped with the knowledge to both execute these techniques ethically during engagements and fortify their organizations against such manipulative strategies.

9.1 Overview of Social Engineering Techniques

Social engineering is a critical component of red team operations, involving the manipulation of individuals to gain unauthorized access to systems or information. Unlike traditional hacking methods that rely on technical exploits, social engineering leverages psychological tactics to deceive individuals into divulging confidential information, performing actions, or bypassing security measures. This chapter provides an overview of social engineering techniques, exploring how they are employed by attackers, the psychology behind these methods, and the implications for cybersecurity.

Understanding Social Engineering

Social engineering refers to the psychological manipulation of people to perform actions or divulge confidential information. This practice exploits human emotions, such as fear, trust, urgency, and curiosity, to trick individuals into compromising security protocols. Given that human error is often the weakest link in security, social engineering remains a prevalent tactic among cybercriminals and is frequently simulated by red teams during security assessments.

Key Techniques in Social Engineering

Phishing

Overview: Phishing is one of the most common and effective social engineering techniques, where attackers send fraudulent communications, typically via email, impersonating a trusted source to trick individuals into revealing sensitive information or downloading malicious software.

Types:

- **Spear Phishing**: Targeting specific individuals or organizations with tailored messages.
- **Whaling**: A form of spear phishing directed at high-profile targets, such as executives.
- **Clone Phishing**: Resending a previously delivered legitimate message with a malicious link or attachment.
- **Example**: An attacker may send an email that appears to be from an employee's bank, prompting them to click a link and enter their login credentials on a fake website.

Pretexting

Overview: Pretexting involves creating a fabricated scenario or impersonating someone to obtain information from the target. This technique requires a certain level of research to create a convincing backstory.

Methods:

- **Assuming Roles**: Pretending to be someone of authority, such as an IT administrator or vendor.
- **Creating Urgency**: Developing a scenario where the target feels pressured to provide information quickly.
- **Example**: An attacker may call an employee claiming to be from the IT department, stating there's an urgent issue that requires their password to resolve.

Baiting

Overview: Baiting is a technique that involves enticing victims with a promise of something appealing to lure them into a trap, often by using physical or digital bait.

Methods:

- **Physical Bait**: Leaving infected USB drives in public places, enticing individuals to pick them up and plug them into their computers.
- **Digital Bait**: Offering free downloads or software that contain malware.
- **Example**: An attacker might leave USB drives labeled "Salary Information" in a company parking lot, hoping that employees will insert them into their work computers.

Tailgating

Overview: Tailgating (or piggybacking) is a physical social engineering technique where an unauthorized person gains access to a restricted area by following an authorized individual.

Methods:

- **Physical Proximity**: Remaining close to an authorized person to slip through a secure door.
- **Exploiting Politeness**: Asking an authorized individual to hold the door open, using social norms against them.
- **Example**: An attacker may wait for an employee to badge into a secure area and then quickly follow them inside without presenting their own credentials.

Vishing

Overview: Vishing (voice phishing) is a social engineering technique conducted over the phone, where attackers manipulate individuals into providing sensitive information or transferring funds.

Methods:

- **Impersonation**: Calling targets while pretending to be a legitimate entity, such as a bank or government agency.
- **Urgency and Fear**: Creating a sense of panic, such as threatening legal action if immediate action isn't taken.
- **Example**: An attacker may call an individual claiming their bank account has been compromised and request immediate verification of account details to prevent further issues.

Social Media Exploitation

Overview: Attackers can leverage social media platforms to gather information about targets or to launch social engineering attacks directly.

Methods:

- **Reconnaissance**: Collecting personal information to create convincing phishing messages.
- **Fake Accounts**: Creating profiles to establish trust and solicit sensitive information from targets.
- **Example**: An attacker might create a fake LinkedIn profile resembling a colleague of the target and then send connection requests, later using the established connection to ask for sensitive information.

Quizzing

Overview: Quizzing involves posing as someone who needs assistance and asking a series of questions to elicit sensitive information from the target.

Methods:

- **Casual Conversation**: Engaging targets in informal discussions to gather information subtly.
- **Leveraging Authority**: Pretending to be a researcher or student seeking data for a project.
- **Example**: An attacker might engage an employee in conversation about company policies, leading them to inadvertently share confidential information.

The Psychology Behind Social Engineering

The success of social engineering attacks lies in their ability to exploit human psychology. Attackers often employ techniques that trigger emotional responses:

- **Fear**: Threats of account closure, job loss, or legal consequences can compel individuals to act quickly without critical thinking.
- **Trust**: Leveraging authority or familiarity can encourage individuals to share information they would normally keep private.

- **Urgency**: Creating a sense of immediacy can lead individuals to bypass security protocols and share sensitive data.

Understanding these psychological triggers enables red teams to simulate effective social engineering attacks, helping organizations recognize their vulnerabilities.

Implications for Cybersecurity

Given the prevalence of social engineering tactics, organizations must prioritize training and awareness programs to mitigate risks. Employees should be educated on recognizing potential social engineering attempts, implementing best practices, and reporting suspicious activities.

Social engineering techniques play a significant role in the success of cyberattacks, relying on the manipulation of human behavior rather than solely on technical vulnerabilities. By understanding and simulating these techniques, red teams can provide valuable insights into organizational weaknesses, ultimately aiding in the development of more robust cybersecurity practices. Organizations must remain vigilant, fostering a culture of awareness and education to combat social engineering threats effectively.

9.2 Conducting Phishing Simulations

Phishing simulations are a vital component of an organization's security awareness training program. They provide a practical approach to educating employees about the dangers of phishing attacks and help to build a robust human firewall against these threats. By simulating real-world phishing scenarios, organizations can assess their vulnerability to such attacks, identify areas for improvement, and ultimately enhance their overall cybersecurity posture. This chapter explores the process of conducting phishing simulations, including planning, execution, and post-simulation analysis.

Understanding Phishing Simulations

Phishing simulations are controlled exercises where employees are targeted with mock phishing emails designed to mimic real phishing attempts. The goal is to evaluate their responses and raise awareness of the tactics used by attackers. These simulations can take various forms, including email phishing, SMS phishing (smishing), and voice phishing (vishing).

Importance of Phishing Simulations

Employee Awareness: Simulations help employees recognize phishing attempts, enhancing their ability to identify and respond to real threats.

Measuring Vulnerability: Organizations can measure their susceptibility to phishing attacks by analyzing the percentage of employees who fall for the simulation.

Improving Incident Response: Phishing simulations can help organizations refine their incident response protocols by identifying gaps in reporting and response practices.

Reinforcing Training: Regular simulations reinforce training programs, keeping security awareness at the forefront of employees' minds.

Planning Phishing Simulations

Define Objectives

- Establish clear goals for the simulation, such as assessing employee awareness, testing incident response procedures, or identifying specific vulnerabilities.
- Determine key performance indicators (KPIs) to evaluate the success of the simulation, such as the percentage of employees who clicked on links or reported the phishing attempt.

Identify the Target Audience

- Determine which groups of employees will be included in the simulation. This can range from all employees to specific departments that handle sensitive data.
- Consider segmenting employees based on their roles and responsibilities, allowing for more targeted scenarios.

Select Simulation Types and Techniques

Choose the types of phishing simulations to conduct, such as:

- **Email Phishing**: Sending fraudulent emails to mimic common phishing tactics.
- **Smishing**: Using SMS messages to simulate phishing attempts.
- **Vishing**: Conducting phone calls to impersonate a legitimate entity and solicit sensitive information.

Consider using multiple techniques to gauge employee awareness across different channels.

Design Realistic Scenarios

- Craft phishing emails or messages that closely resemble real-world attacks, incorporating elements that employees might encounter in their daily work.
- Use psychological triggers such as urgency, fear, or authority to increase the realism of the scenarios.
- Include recognizable company branding to enhance believability, while ensuring that the content aligns with common phishing tactics.

Choose Simulation Tools

- Select phishing simulation tools or platforms that offer pre-built templates, customizable scenarios, and tracking features to measure employee responses.
- Ensure the chosen tools comply with privacy regulations and ethical standards.

Executing Phishing Simulations

Launch the Simulation

- Deploy the phishing simulation to the target audience, ensuring that the timing is appropriate and that employees are unaware of the exercise.
- Monitor the simulation in real-time to track employee interactions, such as clicks on links or responses to the simulated phishing emails.

Collect Data

Gather data on employee responses, including:

- The percentage of employees who clicked on phishing links.
- The number of employees who reported the phishing attempt.
- The time taken to respond to the simulated attack.

Maintain Ethical Standards

- Ensure that the simulation is conducted ethically, respecting employee privacy and dignity.

- Avoid targeting vulnerable employees or using excessively aggressive tactics that may create a hostile work environment.

Post-Simulation Analysis

Analyze Results

- Review the data collected during the simulation to assess employee behavior and identify trends or patterns in responses.
- Calculate KPIs, such as the click-through rate (CTR) and the reporting rate, to evaluate the organization's vulnerability to phishing attacks.

Provide Feedback and Training

- Share the results of the simulation with employees, highlighting areas of concern and positive behaviors.
- Offer additional training resources or workshops to address knowledge gaps and reinforce best practices for recognizing and reporting phishing attempts.

Identify Areas for Improvement

- Use the simulation results to identify specific vulnerabilities within the organization, such as departments that may require additional training or changes in policy.
- Adjust the overall security awareness training program based on the insights gained from the simulation.

Conduct Follow-Up Simulations

- Plan regular phishing simulations to maintain employee awareness and measure improvements over time.
- Gradually increase the complexity of the simulations to challenge employees and reinforce their learning.

Best Practices for Conducting Phishing Simulations

Be Transparent: While employees should not know the specifics of the simulations beforehand, it's essential to be transparent about the organization's commitment to improving security awareness.

Foster a Positive Culture: Create an environment where employees feel comfortable discussing security concerns and reporting potential threats without fear of punishment.

Tailor Scenarios to Your Organization: Customize phishing scenarios to reflect the specific risks and challenges faced by your organization, including industry-specific threats.

Encourage Reporting: Emphasize the importance of reporting suspected phishing attempts, and provide easy-to-use reporting mechanisms to facilitate this process.

Engage Leadership: Involve management in the phishing simulation process to demonstrate the organization's commitment to cybersecurity and set an example for employees.

Conducting phishing simulations is a powerful strategy for enhancing employee awareness and resilience against phishing attacks. By planning, executing, and analyzing these simulations, organizations can gain valuable insights into their vulnerabilities and take proactive steps to bolster their defenses. As cyber threats continue to evolve, ongoing education and training remain critical to fostering a security-conscious culture within the organization, ultimately reducing the risk of successful phishing attempts.

9.3 Awareness Training for Employees

Awareness training for employees is a fundamental aspect of any cybersecurity strategy, and it plays a crucial role in defending against social engineering attacks like phishing, vishing, and other manipulation tactics. Employees are often the first line of defense and, simultaneously, the weakest link if they are not equipped with the right knowledge. This chapter covers the key components of creating an effective security awareness training program, focusing on teaching employees to recognize, resist, and report potential threats, with an emphasis on practical skills and ongoing education.

Importance of Security Awareness Training

With cyberattacks becoming increasingly sophisticated, it is essential for employees to have a strong understanding of cybersecurity basics and their role in safeguarding the organization. Security awareness training empowers employees to:

- **Recognize Threats**: Learn to identify phishing emails, suspicious links, and unusual requests.
- **Understand Their Role**: Employees must realize they are integral to the organization's security, knowing how their actions impact the overall defense.
- **Respond Appropriately**: Training helps employees know what steps to take when they suspect an attack, such as reporting the incident or avoiding malicious actions.
- **Reduce Human Error**: By focusing on habitual behaviors and providing regular reminders, awareness training can help mitigate common mistakes that lead to breaches.

Key Elements of an Awareness Training Program

Foundational Cybersecurity Knowledge

- **Phishing Awareness**: Educate employees about the different types of phishing attacks (e.g., email phishing, smishing, and vishing) and the tactics attackers use, such as impersonating trusted entities or creating a sense of urgency.
- **Password Management**: Stress the importance of strong, unique passwords for every account and introduce concepts like two-factor authentication (2FA) for enhanced security.
- **Recognizing Malware and Suspicious Activity**: Teach employees to identify warning signs of malware, such as slow performance, unusual pop-ups, or unexpected redirects, and the importance of avoiding untrusted downloads.
- **Safe Internet Practices**: Encourage cautious browsing habits, avoiding suspicious links, and verifying the legitimacy of websites before entering credentials or sensitive information.

Simulated Attack Training

- **Phishing Simulations**: As discussed in Chapter 9.2, phishing simulations are a powerful tool in awareness training. By sending simulated phishing emails, employees can practice recognizing and responding to these attacks in a safe, controlled environment.
- **Role-Playing Social Engineering Scenarios**: In addition to phishing simulations, employees can benefit from mock scenarios where attackers attempt to manipulate them in person or over the phone. This helps reinforce how to handle social engineering tactics in real-world situations.

- **Interactive Quizzes and Challenges**: Using gamified challenges, such as quizzes that test employees' ability to spot phishing attempts, makes learning more engaging and encourages participation.

Clear Reporting Channels

- **Encouraging Incident Reporting**: Employees need clear guidance on how to report suspected phishing emails, security incidents, or breaches without hesitation. Establishing a culture where reporting is encouraged and non-punitive is essential.
- **Creating Easy-to-Use Systems**: Whether it's a dedicated email address, helpdesk, or a button within their email system, make it simple for employees to report suspicious activity. Quick, seamless reporting increases the likelihood that employees will take action when necessary.
- **Immediate Feedback**: Provide employees with immediate feedback after they report an issue, confirming whether their suspicion was valid. This reinforces learning and gives employees confidence in their ability to identify threats.

Ongoing Education and Updates

- **Regular Refresher Training**: Cybersecurity awareness cannot be a one-time event. Regular refresher courses, email reminders, and updated training sessions ensure that security practices stay top of mind and evolve alongside emerging threats.
- **Updates on New Threats**: The cyber threat landscape changes rapidly, with new phishing tactics, ransomware, and social engineering methods constantly emerging. Providing updates on the latest trends, either through email bulletins, workshops, or e-learning modules, ensures employees remain vigilant.
- **Mandatory Training for New Employees**: Onboarding processes should include mandatory cybersecurity awareness training for all new employees, making them aware of their responsibilities from day one.

Training Techniques and Approaches

Tailored Training for Different Roles

- **General Employees**: Offer broad training on cybersecurity basics and common threats such as phishing, safe email practices, and general security protocols.

- **High-Risk Roles**: Provide more intensive, specific training for individuals in high-risk roles, such as finance or IT, who might be more frequently targeted by attackers.
- **Executives and Management**: Phishing schemes targeting high-level personnel, known as "whaling," require executives to be particularly aware of their unique exposure. Training should reflect the sophistication of these targeted attacks.

Interactive and Engaging Content

- **E-Learning Modules**: Incorporate video tutorials, interactive modules, and quizzes that allow employees to engage with the material at their own pace. Short, frequent learning sessions are often more effective than long, infrequent lectures.
- **Gamification**: Adding elements of competition, such as leaderboards or rewards for reporting phishing attempts or completing training, motivates employees to participate and learn in a more engaging way.
- **Workshops and Group Exercises**: Hands-on workshops or in-person group training sessions, especially for departments handling sensitive data, provide practical experience in detecting and responding to threats.

Security Awareness Campaigns

- **Email Campaigns**: Regular email campaigns that include tips on spotting phishing attacks, reminders about password hygiene, and updates on the latest cybersecurity threats help keep security top of mind for employees.
- **Posters and Visual Reminders**: Use visual reminders around the workplace, such as posters, infographics, or digital signage, to continuously reinforce key cybersecurity messages.
- **Phishing Newsletters**: Include real-world examples of phishing attempts and breaches that have occurred within the industry or across similar organizations. This creates a sense of urgency and relevance for employees.

Measuring the Effectiveness of Awareness Training

Tracking Metrics

- **Phishing Simulation Results**: After conducting phishing simulations, track how many employees clicked on malicious links or entered sensitive information. This will give insight into the effectiveness of previous training efforts.

- **Reporting Rates**: Monitor how many employees report simulated phishing attacks or other suspicious activities. A higher reporting rate is a strong indicator that awareness is improving.
- **Survey Feedback**: Use post-training surveys to gather feedback from employees on how useful and engaging they found the training. This can help adjust future content and delivery methods.

Assessing Long-Term Behavior Changes

- **Incident Reports**: Track whether the number of real phishing incidents reported by employees increases after awareness training. A rise in reports, especially from departments previously identified as high-risk, may suggest the training has been successful.
- **Security Incidents**: Compare the number of security breaches or incidents caused by human error before and after implementing training programs. A reduction in such incidents is a positive sign of improved security awareness.

Continuous Improvement

- **Reviewing Trends**: Regularly review the training program's effectiveness and adjust it based on new attack trends, simulation results, and employee feedback.
- **Fostering a Security-Conscious Culture**: Over time, the goal is to instill a culture where security awareness becomes second nature for all employees. Continuous education and reinforcement help embed this mindset into the organization's day-to-day operations.

Effective awareness training for employees is an ongoing, proactive defense against social engineering attacks like phishing. By equipping employees with the knowledge and skills they need to recognize threats, report incidents, and act responsibly, organizations can reduce the risk of successful attacks. Continuous training, tailored content, and frequent simulations ensure employees stay vigilant and security-aware in an ever-evolving threat landscape.

Chapter 10: Physical Security Testing

In this chapter, we turn our focus to the often neglected but crucial aspect of cybersecurity: physical security testing. While digital defenses are vital, they can be rendered ineffective if physical access to systems and sensitive information is not adequately controlled. We will begin by examining the principles of physical security and its importance in the overall security posture of an organization. Next, we will discuss various techniques for assessing physical security controls, including security assessments of entry points, surveillance systems, and access control measures. The chapter will also explore methods for gaining unauthorized access, such as social engineering, lock picking, and exploiting vulnerabilities in physical security protocols. Real-world case studies will illustrate the impact of physical security breaches and the lessons learned from these incidents. By the end of this chapter, readers will gain valuable insights into the importance of physical security testing and practical strategies for evaluating and enhancing their organization's physical defenses, ensuring a holistic approach to cybersecurity.

10.1 Assessing Physical Security Controls

In an increasingly digital world, the importance of physical security remains paramount, as many cyber threats can be exacerbated by inadequate physical safeguards. Physical security controls encompass the measures that protect an organization's assets from physical actions and events that could cause damage or loss. This chapter delves into the principles of assessing physical security controls, the methodologies employed in the assessment process, and best practices for enhancing an organization's overall security posture.

Understanding Physical Security Controls

Physical security controls are designed to protect people, property, and information from unauthorized access, damage, or interference. These controls can include:

Access Control Systems: Measures that restrict entry to facilities, such as ID card access, biometric scanners, and security personnel.

Surveillance Systems: Closed-circuit television (CCTV) cameras and monitoring systems used to detect and deter unauthorized activities.

Environmental Controls: Systems that protect against environmental hazards, such as fire suppression systems, temperature controls, and flood prevention measures.

Perimeter Security: Fencing, barriers, and landscaping designed to deter unauthorized access to a facility.

Emergency Response Plans: Procedures and training designed to address incidents such as natural disasters, fire, and active shooter scenarios.

Assessing the effectiveness of these physical security controls is crucial for identifying vulnerabilities and ensuring a comprehensive security strategy.

The Assessment Process

Establishing Assessment Objectives

- Define clear objectives for the physical security assessment, such as identifying vulnerabilities, evaluating compliance with security policies, or measuring the effectiveness of existing controls.
- Involve key stakeholders, including security personnel, IT staff, and upper management, to align on goals and expectations.

Conducting a Security Survey

- **Site Visit**: Conduct a thorough walkthrough of the facility to identify and evaluate the physical security controls in place. This should include a review of entrances, exits, and sensitive areas like server rooms or data centers.
- **Document Current Controls**: Take note of the existing physical security measures, including access control systems, surveillance cameras, alarm systems, and any other relevant infrastructure.
- **Assess Environmental Factors**: Evaluate the location of the facility and its surroundings. Consider factors such as crime rates in the area, natural disaster risks, and proximity to other vulnerable structures.

Identifying Vulnerabilities

- **Weak Points**: Identify areas where security controls may be insufficient or ineffective. Common vulnerabilities include poorly secured entrances, lack of surveillance in critical areas, and inadequate environmental controls.

- **Behavioral Assessment**: Observe employee behaviors and access patterns. This includes assessing whether employees follow security protocols, such as using ID badges or locking doors behind them.
- **Reviewing Incident History**: Analyze previous security incidents or breaches to understand patterns and recurring vulnerabilities that may need to be addressed.

Evaluating Security Policies and Procedures

- Review the organization's physical security policies and procedures to ensure they align with best practices and current industry standards.
- Evaluate the training provided to employees regarding physical security measures, emergency response protocols, and reporting procedures.

Engaging with Security Personnel

- Interview security personnel to understand their perspective on the effectiveness of existing controls and any challenges they face in maintaining security.
- Gather insights on incident response times, communication practices, and the level of training received.

Utilizing Assessment Tools

- Leverage assessment tools and frameworks to evaluate physical security controls systematically. This can include checklists, risk assessment matrices, and compliance evaluation tools.
- Consider using physical security assessment standards such as ASIS International's Physical Security Assessment Standard or the International Organization for Standardization (ISO) standards.

Best Practices for Physical Security Assessment

Regular Assessments

- Conduct physical security assessments on a regular basis to ensure controls remain effective and up-to-date. Consider seasonal assessments to account for varying risks (e.g., holiday crowds, weather-related issues).
- Implement a schedule for routine inspections, with specific attention to areas identified as vulnerable during previous assessments.

Involve All Stakeholders

- Engage a diverse group of stakeholders during the assessment process, including IT staff, human resources, operations, and facility management. Their unique perspectives can help identify vulnerabilities and improve overall security practices.
- Encourage a culture of security awareness across the organization, emphasizing the importance of physical security as part of the broader security strategy.

Document Findings and Recommendations

- Maintain thorough documentation of the assessment process, findings, and recommendations. This documentation can serve as a baseline for future assessments and a reference for improvement efforts.
- Create actionable recommendations based on assessment findings, prioritizing improvements that address the most critical vulnerabilities first.

Follow Up on Remediation Efforts

- After identifying vulnerabilities, ensure that appropriate remediation measures are implemented in a timely manner. This may include upgrading access control systems, enhancing surveillance coverage, or improving employee training.
- Monitor the effectiveness of remediation efforts through follow-up assessments and employee feedback.

Integrate Physical and Cybersecurity Efforts

- Recognize that physical security and cybersecurity are interrelated. Ensure that physical security assessments consider potential cyber vulnerabilities, such as network access points in unsecured areas or physical access to critical IT infrastructure.
- Implement a holistic security strategy that combines physical and cybersecurity measures, fostering collaboration between the two domains.

Assessing physical security controls is a critical component of an organization's overall security strategy. By systematically evaluating existing measures, identifying vulnerabilities, and implementing best practices, organizations can enhance their physical security posture and reduce the risk of incidents that could compromise sensitive assets. As threats continue to evolve, a proactive approach to physical security assessments ensures that organizations remain resilient in the face of potential risks, safeguarding both people and information.

10.2 Techniques for Gaining Unauthorized Access

Unauthorized access to physical spaces poses significant risks to organizations, as it can lead to data breaches, theft of sensitive information, or disruption of operations. Understanding the techniques that attackers might use to gain unauthorized access is essential for organizations to strengthen their physical security measures and protect their assets. This chapter explores various tactics employed by malicious actors to infiltrate physical spaces, highlighting the importance of awareness and proactive defense mechanisms.

Common Techniques for Unauthorized Access

Tailgating and Piggybacking

- **Tailgating**: This technique involves an unauthorized individual following an authorized person through a secure entrance without proper authentication. Attackers often exploit human behavior by taking advantage of the politeness of individuals who hold the door open for them.
- **Piggybacking**: Similar to tailgating, piggybacking occurs when an unauthorized person accompanies an authorized individual, but this method often involves the unauthorized individual asking for permission to enter, creating a perception of legitimacy.
- **Countermeasures**: Implementing stricter access control measures, such as turnstiles, mantraps, and requiring individual identification for entry, can help mitigate these risks. Employee training on not allowing others to follow them through secured areas is also essential.

Social Engineering

- **Pretexting**: In pretexting, attackers create a fabricated scenario to obtain information or gain access. For instance, an attacker may pose as a maintenance worker or IT support, claiming they need access to conduct repairs or updates.
- **Impersonation**: Attackers may impersonate trusted individuals, such as company executives or emergency personnel, to gain access. By using fake credentials or uniforms, they exploit the natural inclination to trust authority figures.

- **Countermeasures**: Organizations should implement strict verification procedures for personnel requesting access, including calling the individual or department the impersonator claims to represent to confirm their legitimacy.

Exploiting Physical Security Weaknesses

- **Open Windows and Doors**: Many attackers look for unsecured points of entry, such as unlocked doors or windows. Organizations often overlook securing these entry points, especially in less-trafficked areas.
- **Faulty or Inoperative Locks**: Malfunctioning locks, broken access control systems, or outdated security technologies can be easily exploited by intruders.
- **Countermeasures**: Regular inspections and maintenance of locks, access points, and security systems are crucial. Establishing policies for securing all entry points, particularly after hours, can help reduce vulnerabilities.

Access Control Bypass Techniques

- **Card Cloning and Duplication**: Attackers can use electronic devices to clone access cards or badges. This method allows them to create duplicates of authorized access credentials, granting them entry to secure areas.
- **Using Deadbolts and Lock Picking**: Skilled attackers can pick locks or use tools to manipulate deadbolts. Although this method requires expertise, it remains a potential threat if physical locks are not designed to resist tampering.
- **Countermeasures**: Implement multifactor authentication (MFA) for access control systems, where users need to provide additional verification beyond a card or code. Regularly updating access control technologies can also help mitigate these risks.

Accessing Unattended Workstations

- **Left Open Workstations**: Employees may leave their computers or secure areas unattended without logging off, providing attackers with easy access to sensitive information or systems.
- **Shoulder Surfing**: Attackers can exploit situations where individuals are entering sensitive information by observing them from a distance, often in public or semi-public spaces.
- **Countermeasures**: Encourage a culture of security awareness by training employees to lock their workstations when not in use and be mindful of their surroundings when entering sensitive information. Implementing automatic screen lock features after a period of inactivity can also help.

Physical Surveillance and Reconnaissance

- **Observation**: Attackers often perform reconnaissance to observe employees' routines, identifying times when access points may be less secure or when employees may be distracted.
- **Documenting Security Protocols**: By observing security personnel, attackers can learn about the timing of security checks, entry processes, and vulnerabilities in the physical security measures.
- **Countermeasures**: Conduct regular security audits and encourage employees to report any suspicious behavior. Use surveillance cameras effectively to monitor access points and employee behavior, reinforcing the perception that the area is being monitored.

Exploiting Emergencies or Unusual Situations

- **Distraction Techniques**: Attackers may create a distraction, such as a fake emergency or an urgent request for assistance, to divert security personnel's attention while they gain access to restricted areas.
- **Emergency Exits and Procedures**: Some attackers may take advantage of emergency exit protocols, entering through doors designated for emergencies, especially during high-traffic events when security protocols may be lax.
- **Countermeasures**: Establish clear protocols for handling emergencies and ensure all employees are trained to recognize and respond to potential distractions or anomalies in security procedures.

The Role of Technology in Physical Security

Access Control Systems

- Modern access control systems use biometric verification, smart cards, and mobile credentials to enhance security. These systems can help mitigate unauthorized access by ensuring that only authorized individuals can enter secure areas.
- Implementing real-time monitoring and alerts for unauthorized access attempts can help security teams respond swiftly to potential breaches.

Surveillance Technologies

- CCTV cameras equipped with advanced analytics can help detect unusual behavior, such as tailgating or loitering, triggering alerts for security personnel to investigate.
- Integrating surveillance systems with access control can provide a comprehensive overview of security incidents and access attempts, allowing for a more effective response.

Environmental Security Controls

- Intrusion detection systems (IDS) and environmental controls, such as temperature sensors and fire alarms, play a crucial role in protecting facilities from unauthorized access and environmental threats.
- Organizations should regularly assess these systems to ensure they function properly and provide adequate coverage of all access points.

Understanding the techniques used to gain unauthorized access to physical spaces is vital for organizations looking to enhance their security measures. By recognizing common vulnerabilities and implementing proactive countermeasures, businesses can significantly reduce the risk of unauthorized access and protect their assets. Continuous training, regular assessments, and leveraging technology are essential components in developing a robust physical security strategy that addresses emerging threats and maintains a secure environment for employees and resources.

10.3 Evaluating the Effectiveness of Physical Security Measures

Evaluating the effectiveness of physical security measures is crucial for organizations aiming to protect their assets, personnel, and sensitive information from unauthorized access and potential threats. A comprehensive evaluation involves assessing existing security controls, identifying vulnerabilities, and ensuring that all measures align with the organization's security objectives. This chapter discusses various methods for evaluating physical security measures, highlighting key performance indicators (KPIs), assessment methodologies, and best practices for maintaining an effective security posture.

Importance of Evaluating Physical Security Measures

- **Identifying Vulnerabilities**: Regular evaluations help identify weaknesses in physical security systems, allowing organizations to address these vulnerabilities proactively.
- **Compliance with Standards**: Evaluations ensure that security measures comply with industry standards and regulatory requirements, reducing the risk of legal liabilities.
- **Resource Optimization**: By assessing the effectiveness of existing measures, organizations can allocate resources more efficiently, prioritizing investments in security technologies and personnel.
- **Continuous Improvement**: A robust evaluation process fosters a culture of continuous improvement, enabling organizations to adapt to evolving threats and refine their security strategies over time.

Key Performance Indicators (KPIs) for Physical Security

To effectively evaluate physical security measures, organizations should establish relevant KPIs that provide quantifiable data on the performance of their security systems. Common KPIs include:

Access Control Effectiveness:

- **Percentage of Unauthorized Access Attempts**: Measure the number of unauthorized access attempts detected by security systems compared to total access attempts. A high percentage indicates effective access control measures.
- **Average Response Time to Access Violations**: Track the average time taken for security personnel to respond to unauthorized access alerts. Short response times indicate a well-trained and efficient security team.

Incident Response Metrics:

- **Number of Security Incidents**: Monitor the frequency and severity of security incidents within a specified period. A decrease in incidents over time may indicate effective security measures.
- **Incident Resolution Time**: Measure the average time taken to resolve security incidents, from detection to resolution. Efficient resolution processes can minimize potential damage.

Surveillance System Performance:

- **Coverage Area**: Evaluate the percentage of critical areas covered by surveillance cameras. Gaps in coverage can indicate potential vulnerabilities.
- **Video Retention Period**: Assess the duration for which surveillance footage is retained. Adequate retention periods are essential for investigating incidents and providing evidence.

Employee Awareness and Training:

- **Training Completion Rates**: Track the percentage of employees who have completed physical security training programs. High completion rates indicate a proactive approach to security awareness.
- **Employee Reporting of Security Breaches**: Measure the number of security breaches reported by employees. Increased reporting suggests that employees are vigilant and engaged in security practices.

Assessment Methodologies

Physical Security Audits:

- Conduct comprehensive audits of physical security measures, assessing the effectiveness of access controls, surveillance systems, and emergency response protocols. Audits should involve reviewing policies, procedures, and security technology.
- Utilize standardized assessment frameworks, such as the ASIS International Physical Security Assessment Standard, to ensure consistency and thoroughness in evaluations.

Testing and Simulation:

- Perform regular penetration testing and red teaming exercises to simulate real-world scenarios where unauthorized access attempts may occur. These tests can uncover vulnerabilities in physical security measures and help organizations understand how security personnel respond to incidents.
- Conduct drills and tabletop exercises to evaluate emergency response protocols. These simulations can help identify gaps in procedures and improve overall readiness.

Surveillance and Monitoring:

- Implement continuous monitoring of surveillance footage to evaluate the effectiveness of camera placements and responsiveness to potential incidents. Analyze footage to identify patterns of suspicious behavior or access attempts.
- Use automated analytics tools that can flag anomalies or unauthorized access attempts, enhancing the efficiency of security monitoring.

Employee Feedback:

- Gather feedback from employees regarding their perceptions of physical security measures. Surveys and interviews can provide insights into the effectiveness of security protocols and areas for improvement.
- Conduct regular focus groups to discuss security concerns and suggestions for enhancing physical security measures. Engaging employees fosters a culture of security awareness and collaboration.

Best Practices for Maintaining Effective Physical Security Measures

Regular Reviews and Updates:

- Schedule periodic reviews of physical security measures to ensure they remain effective in the face of evolving threats. These reviews should assess the adequacy of current technologies and protocols.
- Update security policies and procedures as needed, particularly in response to incidents or changes in the organization's operations.

Investing in Technology:

- Stay informed about emerging security technologies that can enhance physical security measures. Investing in modern access control systems, surveillance technologies, and alarm systems can significantly improve security effectiveness.
- Consider integrating physical security systems with cybersecurity measures for a holistic approach to organizational security.

Employee Training and Engagement:

- Provide ongoing training for employees to keep them informed about physical security policies, emergency procedures, and the importance of reporting suspicious activities. Regular training sessions reinforce security awareness.

- Foster a culture of security by encouraging employees to take ownership of their roles in maintaining security. Recognizing and rewarding proactive security behaviors can enhance engagement.

Collaboration with Local Law Enforcement:

- Establish relationships with local law enforcement agencies to improve response times and coordination during incidents. Regular communication can facilitate information sharing and enhance security preparedness.
- Invite local law enforcement representatives to conduct security assessments or training sessions, providing employees with valuable insights into threat recognition and response.

Creating an Incident Response Plan:

- Develop and maintain a comprehensive incident response plan that outlines procedures for responding to security breaches or emergencies. The plan should be regularly reviewed and updated based on lessons learned from past incidents.
- Ensure that all employees are familiar with the incident response plan and participate in training exercises to reinforce their roles during a security event.

Evaluating the effectiveness of physical security measures is essential for organizations seeking to protect their assets and maintain a secure environment. By establishing clear KPIs, employing assessment methodologies, and adhering to best practices, organizations can continuously improve their physical security posture. Regular evaluations, employee engagement, and investment in modern technologies not only help identify vulnerabilities but also foster a culture of security awareness that enhances overall organizational resilience. In an age where threats continue to evolve, maintaining a proactive and adaptive approach to physical security is vital for safeguarding people and information.

Chapter 11: Reporting and Debriefing

In this chapter, we explore the vital processes of reporting and debriefing following a red team engagement, which serve to communicate findings effectively and foster continuous improvement within an organization. We will begin by discussing the critical components of a well-structured red team report, including the importance of clarity, conciseness, and actionable recommendations. Readers will learn how to categorize findings based on risk levels, prioritize vulnerabilities, and tailor their communication to different stakeholders, ensuring that both technical and non-technical audiences can grasp the implications of the findings. Next, we will delve into the debriefing process, emphasizing the value of collaborative discussions with stakeholders to review results, share insights, and promote a culture of security awareness. This chapter will also cover strategies for conducting productive debriefing sessions, including setting objectives, facilitating open dialogue, and incorporating feedback into future engagements. By the end of this chapter, readers will be equipped with the skills necessary to effectively report on their red team activities and engage stakeholders in meaningful discussions that drive improvements in security practices and overall organizational resilience.

11.1 Structuring the Red Team Report

A well-structured Red Team report is crucial for communicating findings, recommendations, and the overall impact of a Red Team engagement to stakeholders within an organization. It serves not only as a document detailing the team's activities and results but also as a strategic tool for improving the organization's security posture. This chapter provides an overview of the essential components and structure of a Red Team report, ensuring it is both comprehensive and clear for its intended audience.

Purpose of the Red Team Report

The primary purpose of a Red Team report is to document the findings from the Red Team engagement and provide actionable insights to strengthen an organization's security posture. It serves several key functions:

- **Communication**: Conveying findings, vulnerabilities, and security weaknesses to stakeholders in a clear and concise manner.
- **Awareness**: Raising awareness about the current threat landscape and the organization's susceptibility to specific attack vectors.

- **Actionable Recommendations**: Offering practical recommendations to mitigate identified vulnerabilities and improve overall security measures.
- **Documentation**: Providing a formal record of the engagement that can be referenced in future assessments and security planning.

Essential Components of the Red Team Report

To effectively communicate findings and recommendations, a Red Team report should be structured into several key sections. Below is a recommended outline for structuring a comprehensive Red Team report:

Executive Summary

- **Overview of the Engagement**: A brief summary of the Red Team engagement, including objectives, scope, and duration.
- **Key Findings**: Highlight the most significant vulnerabilities and findings uncovered during the engagement.
- **Recommendations**: A concise list of prioritized recommendations to address the identified weaknesses.

Engagement Objectives

- **Purpose of the Engagement**: Clearly outline the goals of the Red Team exercise, such as testing specific security controls or simulating real-world attack scenarios.
- **Scope of Work**: Detail the boundaries of the engagement, including which systems, networks, and physical locations were tested, as well as any limitations or exclusions.

Methodology

- **Approach Used**: Describe the methodologies and frameworks employed during the Red Team engagement, including any specific tools or techniques utilized.
- **Phases of Engagement**: Outline the key phases of the engagement, such as reconnaissance, exploitation, post-exploitation, and reporting.

Findings and Vulnerabilities

- **Detailed Findings**: Present detailed descriptions of vulnerabilities discovered during the engagement, including technical details, screenshots, and relevant data to support the findings.
- **Risk Assessment**: Assess the risk associated with each finding, categorizing vulnerabilities based on their potential impact and exploitability (e.g., critical, high, medium, low).
- **Attack Vectors**: Describe the attack vectors used to exploit vulnerabilities and gain unauthorized access, including any relevant context about the simulated threats.

Impact Analysis

- **Potential Consequences**: Analyze the potential impact of each vulnerability if exploited by an attacker, including data breaches, operational disruption, or reputational damage.
- **Likelihood of Exploitation**: Discuss the likelihood of each vulnerability being exploited in a real-world scenario, taking into account existing defenses and security controls.

Recommendations

- **Actionable Steps**: Provide specific, actionable recommendations to remediate identified vulnerabilities and improve security controls.
- **Prioritization**: Prioritize recommendations based on risk assessment findings, helping stakeholders focus on the most critical areas for improvement.
- **Resources Required**: Identify any resources needed for implementation, such as personnel, training, or technology investments.

Conclusion

- **Summary of Engagement**: Summarize the key findings and recommendations from the engagement.
- **Future Considerations**: Discuss any implications for future security assessments or ongoing security improvements.

Appendices

- **Technical Details:** Include any technical documentation, configurations, or additional data that supports the findings.

- **References**: Provide a list of references for methodologies, tools, or frameworks used during the engagement.
- **Glossary of Terms**: Define any technical terms or acronyms used throughout the report to enhance clarity for non-technical stakeholders.

Best Practices for Writing the Red Team Report

Clarity and Conciseness: Ensure that the report is clear and concise, using straightforward language to communicate findings and recommendations effectively. Avoid jargon or overly technical terms unless necessary, and provide explanations where needed.

Visual Aids: Use visual aids such as graphs, charts, and screenshots to illustrate key findings and data. Visuals can help simplify complex information and make the report more engaging for readers.

Tailored Audience Focus: Consider the audience for the report and tailor the content accordingly. Executives may require a high-level overview, while technical teams may need detailed findings and technical recommendations.

Action Orientation: Emphasize actionable recommendations and next steps throughout the report. Providing clear guidance on how to address vulnerabilities reinforces the purpose of the Red Team engagement.

Review and Feedback: Before finalizing the report, solicit feedback from team members and stakeholders. Conduct a thorough review to ensure accuracy and completeness of findings and recommendations.

A well-structured Red Team report is essential for effectively communicating findings and recommendations to stakeholders. By following a clear and comprehensive outline, organizations can ensure that the report serves as a valuable tool for enhancing their security posture. Through careful evaluation of vulnerabilities, actionable recommendations, and an emphasis on clear communication, a Red Team report can facilitate informed decision-making and promote continuous improvement in security practices.

11.2 Effective Communication of Findings

Effective communication of findings from a Red Team engagement is critical for ensuring that stakeholders understand the vulnerabilities discovered, their implications, and the necessary actions required to mitigate risks. The process involves not only delivering technical information but also ensuring it is accessible and actionable for diverse audiences, from technical staff to executive leadership. This chapter discusses strategies for communicating findings effectively, emphasizing clarity, relevance, and engagement.

Importance of Effective Communication

- **Understanding Risks**: Clear communication helps stakeholders grasp the severity of vulnerabilities and the associated risks to the organization, facilitating informed decision-making.
- **Building Trust**: Transparent reporting fosters trust between the Red Team and stakeholders, reinforcing the idea that the findings are intended to improve security rather than assign blame.
- **Encouraging Action**: When findings are communicated effectively, stakeholders are more likely to take appropriate actions to address vulnerabilities, leading to tangible improvements in security posture.

Strategies for Effective Communication

Know Your Audience

- **Tailored Messaging**: Different stakeholders have varying levels of technical expertise and interests. Tailor the report and presentations to suit each audience:
- **Executives and Management**: Focus on high-level summaries, emphasizing business impact, risk assessment, and strategic recommendations.
- **Technical Teams**: Provide detailed findings, technical descriptions, and specific remediation steps. Use technical language and include data that supports your conclusions.
- **Consider Diverse Perspectives**: Engage with various departments, such as IT, operations, and compliance, to understand their concerns and priorities, allowing for more effective communication.

Utilize Clear and Concise Language

- **Avoid Jargon**: Minimize technical jargon when addressing non-technical stakeholders. Instead, use plain language and provide explanations for necessary technical terms.

- **Be Concise**: Keep the communication succinct, focusing on key findings and actionable recommendations. Long-winded explanations can lead to confusion and disengagement.

Organize Findings Logically

- **Structured Presentation**: Present findings in a logical order, grouping similar vulnerabilities or issues together. A structured format helps stakeholders follow the narrative and understand the connections between different findings.
- **Use Clear Headings and Subheadings**: Clearly labeled sections improve readability and allow stakeholders to quickly locate specific information relevant to their concerns.

Incorporate Visual Aids

- **Charts and Graphs**: Use visual representations to illustrate key data points, trends, and comparisons. Visual aids can simplify complex information and make it more digestible.
- **Screenshots and Diagrams**: Incorporate screenshots of vulnerabilities or network diagrams to provide visual context. This can enhance understanding and retention of key findings.

Highlight Key Findings and Recommendations

- **Executive Summary**: Start with an executive summary that encapsulates the most critical findings and recommendations. This allows busy executives to quickly grasp the overall picture.
- **Prioritize Recommendations**: Clearly indicate which recommendations are most critical and should be addressed first. Use a prioritization scheme (e.g., high, medium, low) to help stakeholders focus on the most pressing issues.

Facilitate Engagement and Discussion

- **Interactive Presentations**: When presenting findings, encourage questions and discussions to clarify any uncertainties and engage stakeholders in the conversation.
- **Workshops and Training Sessions**: Organize workshops to delve deeper into findings, offering hands-on training or simulations that illustrate potential attack scenarios and corresponding defenses.

Provide Actionable Next Steps

- **Clear Remediation Guidance**: Offer specific, actionable steps for addressing identified vulnerabilities, including responsible parties, timelines, and resources needed for implementation.
- **Follow-Up**: Establish a follow-up process to track the progress of remediation efforts and provide ongoing support to stakeholders in implementing recommendations.

Document Everything

- **Comprehensive Reporting**: Ensure that all findings, methodologies, and recommendations are well documented in the final report. This serves as a reference for stakeholders and a record of the engagement.
- **Version Control**: Maintain version control for reports and presentations, allowing stakeholders to access the most current information and any updates on findings or recommendations.

Overcoming Communication Challenges

- **Technical Complexity**: Communicating complex technical findings to non-technical stakeholders can be challenging. To overcome this, use analogies or real-world examples to explain concepts, making them more relatable and understandable.
- **Resistance to Change**: Some stakeholders may resist acknowledging vulnerabilities or implementing recommendations. Address this by framing discussions around risk management and the potential impacts of not addressing identified issues.
- **Time Constraints**: Stakeholders may have limited time to engage with findings. To counter this, prioritize key messages and provide concise summaries, allowing stakeholders to absorb essential information quickly.

Effective communication of findings from a Red Team engagement is essential for driving security improvements and fostering a culture of risk awareness within an organization. By tailoring messages to diverse audiences, using clear language, and presenting information logically, Red Teams can ensure their findings resonate with stakeholders. Incorporating visual aids, emphasizing actionable recommendations, and facilitating engagement further enhance the effectiveness of communication efforts. Ultimately, the goal is to empower stakeholders to take meaningful actions based on

Red Team findings, leading to a more robust security posture and improved resilience against future threats.

11.3 Conducting Debriefs with Stakeholders

Conducting debriefs with stakeholders after a Red Team engagement is a vital step in translating findings into actionable improvements for an organization's security posture. These sessions provide an opportunity to discuss the outcomes of the engagement, address questions or concerns, and collaboratively develop a plan for remediation. This chapter explores the importance of debriefing, best practices for effective sessions, and strategies to ensure that stakeholders are engaged and informed.

Importance of Stakeholder Debriefs

- **Fostering Communication**: Debriefs create a platform for open dialogue between the Red Team and stakeholders, encouraging transparent communication regarding findings, implications, and next steps.
- **Building Relationships**: Regular debriefing sessions help build trust and rapport between the Red Team and organizational stakeholders, promoting a collaborative approach to security improvements.
- **Clarifying Findings**: Stakeholders may have questions or misunderstandings about the findings reported by the Red Team. Debriefs provide an opportunity to clarify technical details and the context of the vulnerabilities discovered.
- **Encouraging Ownership**: Engaging stakeholders in debriefs fosters a sense of ownership over security measures. By actively participating in discussions about vulnerabilities and solutions, stakeholders are more likely to commit to necessary changes.

Best Practices for Conducting Effective Debriefs

Preparation is Key

- **Identify Participants**: Determine who should be present at the debriefing session. This may include executives, IT personnel, compliance officers, and other relevant stakeholders.
- **Develop an Agenda**: Create a clear agenda outlining the topics to be discussed, including key findings, recommendations, and action items. Share the agenda with participants in advance to ensure everyone is prepared.

- **Gather Materials**: Compile necessary materials, such as the final report, presentation slides, and any supplementary data or visuals that will help communicate findings effectively.

Set a Positive Tone

- **Focus on Improvement**: Frame the debrief as an opportunity for improvement rather than a critique of past performance. Emphasize that the goal is to enhance security measures and protect the organization.
- **Encourage Participation**: Foster an inclusive environment where all stakeholders feel comfortable asking questions and sharing their perspectives. Encourage participation by inviting input and feedback throughout the session.

Present Key Findings Clearly

- **Use Visuals**: Leverage visual aids such as charts, graphs, and screenshots to illustrate key findings. Visuals can enhance understanding and engagement, making complex information more accessible.
- **Summarize Findings**: Begin the debrief with a high-level summary of the key findings and vulnerabilities identified during the engagement. This overview sets the stage for more detailed discussions later.

Facilitate Discussion

- **Open the Floor for Questions**: After presenting key findings, invite stakeholders to ask questions and discuss their concerns. Be prepared to address inquiries regarding specific vulnerabilities, the likelihood of exploitation, and potential impacts.
- **Encourage Collaboration**: Engage stakeholders in collaborative discussions about potential solutions and remediation strategies. This collaborative approach fosters a sense of ownership and commitment to implementing changes.

Prioritize Recommendations

- **Highlight Critical Recommendations**: Focus on the most critical recommendations that address high-risk vulnerabilities first. Clearly explain the rationale behind prioritization to help stakeholders understand the urgency of addressing specific issues.

- **Assign Responsibility**: Discuss who will be responsible for implementing each recommendation and establish timelines for remediation. Assigning accountability helps ensure that actions are taken in a timely manner.

Document Outcomes

- **Record Key Points**: Document key discussion points, decisions made, and action items during the debrief. This documentation serves as a reference for follow-up and accountability.
- **Distribute Meeting Minutes**: Share meeting minutes with all participants after the debrief. This keeps everyone informed about what was discussed and ensures alignment on next steps.

Follow Up

- **Establish Check-In Points**: Schedule follow-up meetings to track progress on action items and address any new concerns that may arise. Regular check-ins reinforce accountability and demonstrate a commitment to continuous improvement.
- **Provide Additional Support**: Offer resources or support to stakeholders as they implement recommendations. This may include additional training, access to tools, or guidance on remediation strategies.

Engaging Different Stakeholders

Executives and Management: Focus discussions on the business implications of findings, such as potential financial impacts, regulatory compliance, and reputational risks. Use strategic language that aligns with organizational goals.

IT and Security Teams: Dive into technical details, discussing specific vulnerabilities, exploitation techniques, and recommendations for remediation. Provide clear guidance on how to address the identified weaknesses.

Non-Technical Stakeholders: Simplify technical jargon and focus on the broader implications of the findings. Use analogies or real-world examples to help non-technical stakeholders understand the importance of addressing vulnerabilities.

Cross-Functional Teams: Engage representatives from various departments to foster a holistic approach to security. Encourage cross-functional collaboration in developing and implementing remediation strategies.

Conducting debriefs with stakeholders is a critical component of the Red Team engagement process. By fostering open communication, clarifying findings, and encouraging collaboration, organizations can effectively translate Red Team findings into actionable improvements. Preparation, clear presentation of findings, facilitation of discussions, and diligent follow-up are essential for successful debriefing sessions. Ultimately, engaging stakeholders in meaningful discussions about vulnerabilities and remediation strategies helps strengthen an organization's security posture and fosters a culture of continuous improvement in cybersecurity practices.

Chapter 12: Lessons Learned and Continuous Improvement

In this chapter, we emphasize the importance of lessons learned and the principle of continuous improvement within the context of red teaming. Following a red team engagement, the ability to analyze outcomes and extract actionable insights is crucial for enhancing an organization's security posture. We will begin by discussing how to conduct a thorough review of red team activities, including evaluating successes, challenges, and areas for growth. Readers will learn effective methodologies for capturing and documenting lessons learned, ensuring that valuable insights are not lost but rather integrated into future planning and execution. Additionally, we will explore the role of feedback loops in promoting continuous improvement, highlighting how organizations can adapt their security strategies based on findings from red team exercises and evolving threat landscapes. This chapter will also cover the importance of fostering a culture of learning within security teams, encouraging open discussions about vulnerabilities and the lessons derived from engagements. By the end of this chapter, readers will understand how to leverage lessons learned as a powerful tool for driving ongoing enhancements in their red teaming efforts and overall cybersecurity practices.

12.1 Analyzing Engagement Outcomes

Analyzing engagement outcomes is a crucial phase in the Red Team process that directly influences an organization's security posture. It involves assessing the results of a Red Team engagement to determine the effectiveness of security measures, identify areas for improvement, and ensure that lessons learned are integrated into future security strategies. This chapter outlines the significance of outcome analysis, key metrics to evaluate, and methodologies for conducting a thorough assessment of engagement results.

Importance of Analyzing Engagement Outcomes

- **Understanding Security Gaps**: By analyzing engagement outcomes, organizations can gain insights into existing security weaknesses, enabling them to prioritize remediation efforts effectively.
- **Evaluating Effectiveness**: Outcome analysis allows organizations to evaluate the effectiveness of their security controls and policies, determining whether they are adequate in mitigating potential threats.

- **Informing Future Engagements**: Insights gained from analyzing past engagements can inform the planning and execution of future Red Team operations, leading to more comprehensive assessments and a stronger security posture.
- **Enhancing Organizational Learning**: Engaging in outcome analysis fosters a culture of continuous improvement by encouraging teams to learn from past experiences, adapt to evolving threats, and enhance overall security practices.

Key Metrics for Analyzing Outcomes

To effectively analyze engagement outcomes, organizations should focus on several key metrics that provide insights into the engagement's success and areas for improvement:

Vulnerabilities Identified

- **Number of Vulnerabilities**: Track the total number of vulnerabilities discovered during the engagement, categorized by severity (e.g., critical, high, medium, low).
- **Types of Vulnerabilities**: Analyze the types of vulnerabilities found (e.g., technical, procedural, human factors) to identify patterns and recurring issues that need to be addressed.

Exploitability Assessment

- **Successful Exploits**: Measure the number of successful exploits achieved by the Red Team compared to the total number of attempts. This metric helps assess the effectiveness of existing defenses.
- **Time to Exploit**: Evaluate the time taken to exploit each vulnerability, as well as the methods used. This can provide insights into how quickly attackers can gain access and the effectiveness of detection mechanisms.

Detection and Response Metrics

- **Detection Rates**: Assess the rate at which security tools and personnel detected Red Team activities during the engagement. High detection rates indicate robust monitoring and alerting capabilities.
- **Response Times**: Measure the time taken for the organization to respond to detected threats. This includes assessing how quickly teams could react to mitigate the risks posed by the Red Team's actions.

Impact Analysis

- **Business Impact Assessment**: Evaluate the potential business impact of the vulnerabilities identified. This includes considering financial implications, operational disruption, and reputational damage.
- **Risk Reduction**: Assess the degree to which vulnerabilities, if left unaddressed, could expose the organization to risk. This helps prioritize remediation efforts based on potential consequences.

Stakeholder Engagement and Awareness

- **Feedback from Stakeholders**: Collect feedback from stakeholders regarding their understanding of the findings and their perceptions of the Red Team engagement's value. This can provide insights into how effectively the findings were communicated.
- **Awareness Training Effectiveness**: Measure the impact of any awareness training conducted post-engagement. Assess whether employees demonstrate increased awareness of security practices and vulnerabilities.

Methodologies for Analyzing Outcomes

To conduct a thorough analysis of engagement outcomes, organizations can adopt several methodologies:

Post-Engagement Review

- **Conduct Review Sessions**: Organize review sessions with the Red Team and stakeholders to discuss findings, successes, challenges, and lessons learned. This collaborative approach fosters an inclusive analysis and encourages diverse perspectives.
- **Identify Patterns**: Analyze findings across multiple engagements to identify recurring vulnerabilities and trends, which can inform future security strategies.

Root Cause Analysis (RCA)

- **Investigate Vulnerabilities**: For each identified vulnerability, conduct a root cause analysis to understand the underlying reasons why it existed. This may involve examining processes, technology, and human factors that contributed to the vulnerability.

- **Develop Corrective Actions**: Based on the RCA, develop corrective actions to address root causes and prevent similar vulnerabilities from arising in the future.

Comparative Analysis

- **Benchmarking Against Standards**: Compare engagement outcomes against industry standards, frameworks, and best practices to evaluate performance. This can help organizations identify gaps and areas for improvement.
- **Evaluate Against Previous Engagements**: Analyze outcomes from previous Red Team engagements to measure progress over time. This can provide insights into the effectiveness of implemented security measures and initiatives.

Quantitative and Qualitative Assessment

- **Quantitative Metrics:** Utilize quantitative metrics (e.g., number of vulnerabilities, detection rates) to provide objective assessments of engagement outcomes.
- **Qualitative Insights**: Supplement quantitative data with qualitative insights from stakeholder feedback and discussions. This can enrich the analysis and highlight areas that may not be captured by metrics alone.

Analyzing engagement outcomes is a critical step in the Red Team process that enables organizations to understand their security posture, identify vulnerabilities, and drive improvements. By focusing on key metrics, employing effective methodologies, and fostering collaboration among stakeholders, organizations can derive valuable insights from Red Team engagements. This process not only enhances security measures but also promotes a culture of continuous improvement, ensuring that organizations are better prepared to defend against evolving threats in the cybersecurity landscape. Ultimately, thorough outcome analysis is instrumental in transforming Red Team findings into actionable strategies that enhance resilience and security across the organization.

12.2 Incorporating Feedback into Security Practices

Incorporating feedback into security practices is a critical step in enhancing an organization's cybersecurity posture. After a Red Team engagement, stakeholders provide valuable insights that can lead to significant improvements in security measures and processes. This chapter explores the importance of feedback, methods for collecting and analyzing it, and strategies for effectively integrating it into ongoing security practices.

Importance of Incorporating Feedback

- **Continuous Improvement**: Feedback from stakeholders helps identify areas where security measures can be strengthened, leading to a culture of continuous improvement. By regularly incorporating feedback, organizations can adapt to emerging threats and evolving business needs.
- **Reinforcing Accountability**: Engaging stakeholders in feedback discussions reinforces a sense of accountability for security practices. When team members see their feedback valued and acted upon, they are more likely to take ownership of security measures and practices.
- **Enhancing Security Awareness**: Feedback sessions often reveal knowledge gaps or misconceptions about security policies and procedures. Addressing these gaps through training and awareness initiatives can improve the overall security posture of the organization.
- **Aligning Security Practices with Business Objectives**: Incorporating stakeholder feedback ensures that security practices align with the organization's goals and objectives. By understanding the business context, security teams can prioritize initiatives that deliver the most significant value.

Methods for Collecting Feedback

Surveys and Questionnaires

- **Post-Engagement Surveys**: Distribute surveys to stakeholders after the Red Team engagement to gather their opinions on the findings, communication effectiveness, and perceived value of the engagement.
- **Quantitative and Qualitative Questions**: Include both quantitative rating scales and open-ended qualitative questions to capture a range of feedback.

Focus Groups and Workshops

- **Organize Focus Groups**: Conduct focus groups with representatives from different departments to gather collective insights and foster discussions around findings and recommendations.
- **Interactive Workshops**: Host workshops that encourage collaborative problem-solving and brainstorming sessions. This format allows stakeholders to express their thoughts and contribute ideas for improvements.

One-on-One Interviews

- **Conduct Interviews**: Schedule interviews with key stakeholders to gather in-depth feedback on specific findings and their implications. One-on-one conversations can lead to more candid discussions and nuanced insights.
- **Tailor Questions**: Prepare questions that address specific concerns or interests relevant to the stakeholder's role, ensuring that the feedback is relevant and actionable.

Feedback Mechanisms

- **Implement Anonymous Channels**: Establish anonymous channels for stakeholders to provide feedback, ensuring they feel comfortable expressing concerns or suggestions without fear of repercussions.
- **Regular Check-Ins**: Schedule periodic check-ins with stakeholders to gather ongoing feedback on security practices and any changes implemented based on previous engagements.

Analyzing Feedback

Identify Common Themes

- **Categorize Feedback**: Organize feedback into categories such as communication effectiveness, vulnerability management, training needs, and policy gaps. This categorization helps identify patterns and areas requiring attention.
- **Look for Recurring Issues**: Analyze feedback for recurring themes or issues that may indicate systemic problems in security practices. Addressing these can lead to significant improvements.

Prioritize Feedback

- **Assess Impact and Feasibility**: Prioritize feedback based on the potential impact on security posture and the feasibility of implementation. Focus on changes that can be made quickly and that provide the most significant benefit.
- **Engage Stakeholders in Prioritization**: Involve stakeholders in the prioritization process to ensure that their concerns are addressed in a way that aligns with organizational goals and resource availability.

Document Findings and Actions

- **Maintain Records**: Document all feedback received, analyses conducted, and actions taken in response. This documentation serves as a reference for future engagements and demonstrates a commitment to continuous improvement.
- **Track Changes Over Time**: Establish a system for tracking changes made in response to feedback, allowing organizations to evaluate the effectiveness of implemented changes over time.

Strategies for Integrating Feedback into Security Practices

Develop Action Plans

- **Create Actionable Roadmaps**: Develop clear action plans outlining how feedback will be addressed, including timelines, responsibilities, and resource allocations. Ensure that these plans are realistic and achievable.
- **Communicate Action Plans**: Share action plans with stakeholders to keep them informed about how their feedback is being incorporated into security practices.

Update Policies and Procedures

- **Revise Security Policies**: Based on feedback, update security policies and procedures to address identified gaps or weaknesses. Ensure that changes are communicated to all relevant stakeholders.
- **Establish Standard Operating Procedures (SOPs)**: Create or update SOPs to reflect best practices and incorporate lessons learned from feedback. This helps standardize security practices across the organization.

Implement Training and Awareness Programs

- **Tailor Training Initiatives**: Develop training programs based on feedback about knowledge gaps and areas needing improvement. Tailor content to address specific vulnerabilities and promote best practices.
- **Enhance Security Awareness Campaigns**: Use feedback to inform security awareness campaigns, ensuring that messages resonate with employees and address common misconceptions.

Encourage a Culture of Feedback

- **Promote Openness**: Foster a culture that values feedback and encourages employees to share their thoughts and suggestions on security practices continuously. This culture of openness can lead to ongoing improvements and innovation.

- **Recognize Contributions**: Acknowledge and celebrate contributions from employees who provide valuable feedback. Recognition can motivate others to participate in feedback initiatives.

Incorporating feedback into security practices is essential for enhancing an organization's cybersecurity posture and promoting a culture of continuous improvement. By systematically collecting, analyzing, and integrating feedback from stakeholders, organizations can identify vulnerabilities, reinforce accountability, and align security practices with business objectives. Methods such as surveys, focus groups, and one-on-one interviews provide opportunities for meaningful stakeholder engagement. Ultimately, organizations that embrace feedback as a tool for growth will be better equipped to adapt to evolving threats and improve their overall security effectiveness.

12.3 Evolving the Red Team Approach

Evolving the Red Team approach is essential for organizations to stay ahead of emerging threats and to continuously enhance their cybersecurity posture. As cyber threats become more sophisticated and adversaries adopt new tactics, techniques, and procedures (TTPs), Red Teams must adapt their methodologies to provide relevant and effective assessments. This chapter discusses the need for evolution in the Red Team approach, key drivers for change, strategies for adaptation, and the importance of fostering innovation in Red Team operations.

The Need for Evolution in Red Teaming

Dynamic Threat Landscape: The cybersecurity landscape is constantly evolving, with new vulnerabilities, attack vectors, and threat actors emerging regularly. Red Teams must adapt to these changes to effectively simulate real-world attacks and provide meaningful insights to organizations.

Increasing Complexity: As organizations adopt new technologies (e.g., cloud computing, Internet of Things, artificial intelligence), the attack surface expands, making it essential for Red Teams to evolve their strategies to address these complexities.

Adversarial Innovation: Cyber adversaries are continually innovating, utilizing advanced techniques such as machine learning, social engineering, and multi-vector attacks. Red Teams must keep pace with these advancements to remain relevant and effective in their assessments.

Regulatory and Compliance Requirements: Evolving regulatory landscapes may require organizations to update their security practices and assessments regularly. Red Teams must adapt their methodologies to meet these changing compliance standards and ensure that organizations can demonstrate effective security measures.

Key Drivers for Evolving the Red Team Approach

Feedback from Engagements: Analyzing outcomes and stakeholder feedback from past engagements provides valuable insights into the effectiveness of current methodologies and highlights areas for improvement. Continuous learning from these experiences is crucial for evolving Red Team practices.

Industry Trends and Threat Intelligence: Staying informed about industry trends, emerging threats, and best practices is vital for evolving Red Team operations. Leveraging threat intelligence can help teams understand the tactics used by real-world adversaries and adapt their simulations accordingly.

Technological Advancements: Innovations in technology can enhance Red Team capabilities. By adopting new tools and techniques, Red Teams can improve their ability to conduct realistic simulations, gather intelligence, and automate processes.

Cross-Functional Collaboration: Engaging with other departments, such as incident response, blue teams, and compliance, can provide a broader perspective on security challenges and facilitate a more comprehensive approach to evolving Red Team practices.

Strategies for Evolving the Red Team Approach

Adopting Agile Methodologies

- **Iterative Planning and Execution**: Implement agile principles in Red Team operations to allow for iterative planning, execution, and assessment of engagements. This flexibility enables teams to adapt quickly to changing threats and stakeholder needs.
- **Continuous Feedback Loops**: Establish mechanisms for continuous feedback throughout the engagement process, allowing teams to adjust their strategies in real-time based on emerging findings.

Integrating Threat Intelligence

- **Utilize Threat Intelligence Platforms**: Leverage threat intelligence platforms to gather and analyze data on emerging threats, adversary tactics, and vulnerabilities. This intelligence can inform Red Team planning and execution.
- **Conduct Threat Modeling**: Integrate threat modeling exercises into Red Team operations to identify potential attack vectors and prioritize areas for focused engagement.

Enhancing Technical Skills and Knowledge

- **Continuous Training and Development**: Invest in ongoing training and development for Red Team members to ensure they stay current with the latest tools, techniques, and trends in the cybersecurity landscape.
- **Cross-Training**: Encourage cross-training among team members in different areas of cybersecurity (e.g., incident response, blue teaming) to foster a more holistic understanding of security challenges.

Embracing Automation and Tooling

- **Utilize Automation Tools**: Implement automation tools to streamline processes such as reconnaissance, vulnerability scanning, and reporting. Automation can improve efficiency and enable Red Teams to focus on higher-value activities.
- **Develop Custom Tools**: Create or leverage custom tools that simulate advanced adversarial techniques, improving the realism of Red Team engagements and providing organizations with actionable insights.

Fostering Collaboration with Blue Teams

- **Conduct Purple Team Exercises**: Establish collaboration between Red Teams and Blue Teams through purple team exercises, which involve joint engagements that promote knowledge sharing and improve overall security effectiveness.
- **Share Insights and Findings**: After engagements, share insights and findings with Blue Teams to facilitate learning and improve defense strategies. This collaborative approach helps create a more integrated security posture.

Expanding Engagement Scope

- **Include Non-Technical Factors**: Evolve the scope of engagements to include non-technical factors such as social engineering, physical security assessments, and insider threats. This holistic approach ensures that organizations are prepared to address a wide range of vulnerabilities.
- **Simulate Real-World Scenarios**: Incorporate realistic scenarios that reflect actual attack patterns seen in the threat landscape, enabling organizations to understand their vulnerabilities in context and prioritize remediation efforts accordingly.

Fostering Innovation in Red Team Operations

Encourage a Culture of Experimentation

- **Pilot New Approaches**: Create an environment where Red Team members feel empowered to pilot new approaches and techniques without fear of failure. Encouraging experimentation can lead to innovative solutions that enhance engagement outcomes.
- **Conduct Post-Mortems**: After engagements, conduct post-mortem analyses to evaluate what worked well, what didn't, and how future engagements can be improved. This reflective process fosters a culture of learning and innovation.

Incorporate Emerging Technologies

- **Explore AI and Machine Learning**: Investigate the use of artificial intelligence and machine learning in Red Team operations, such as automating threat detection, improving reconnaissance capabilities, and enhancing simulation realism.
- **Leverage Virtual and Augmented Reality**: Consider incorporating virtual and augmented reality technologies for training and simulation exercises, providing immersive environments for Red Team members to practice their skills.

Stay Connected with the Community

- **Participate in Industry Conferences**: Encourage Red Team members to attend cybersecurity conferences, workshops, and seminars to stay informed about the latest trends, tools, and techniques in the field.
- **Engage in Information Sharing**: Collaborate with other organizations and industry groups to share insights, experiences, and best practices. This collective knowledge can drive innovation and enhance overall security capabilities.

Evolving the Red Team approach is essential for organizations to effectively combat the ever-changing cybersecurity landscape. By recognizing the need for evolution, leveraging key drivers for change, and implementing strategies for adaptation, Red Teams can enhance their capabilities and deliver valuable insights to organizations. Fostering a culture of innovation and collaboration not only strengthens Red Team operations but also improves the overall security posture of the organization. As cyber threats continue to evolve, so too must the strategies and methodologies employed by Red Teams to ensure that they remain a vital component of effective cybersecurity practices.

Chapter 13: Tools of the Trade

In this chapter, we take a comprehensive look at the essential tools and technologies that empower red teamers to execute their engagements effectively and efficiently. We will begin by categorizing the various tools used in red teaming, including those for reconnaissance, exploitation, post-exploitation, and reporting. Each category will highlight specific tools, both open-source and commercial, that are widely utilized in the industry. Readers will gain insights into the features and functionalities of popular tools such as Nmap, Metasploit, Burp Suite, and others, providing a practical understanding of how these tools can be applied in real-world scenarios. Additionally, we will discuss the importance of tool selection based on specific engagement objectives and organizational requirements, emphasizing the need for continuous evaluation and adaptation as threats evolve. This chapter will also introduce the concept of setting up a red team lab, offering guidance on creating an environment for testing tools, practicing techniques, and enhancing skills. By the end of this chapter, readers will be well-equipped with knowledge of the essential tools of the trade, enabling them to effectively conduct red team operations and stay ahead of emerging cyber threats.

13.1 Overview of Essential Red Team Tools

In the field of cybersecurity, Red Teams play a critical role in assessing and improving an organization's security posture by simulating real-world attacks. To effectively conduct these assessments, Red Teams rely on a variety of specialized tools designed for various aspects of the testing process. This chapter provides an overview of essential Red Team tools, categorizing them based on their functionality and discussing their key features, use cases, and benefits.

Categories of Red Team Tools

Reconnaissance Tools

Purpose: Reconnaissance tools are used to gather intelligence about the target organization, identifying potential attack vectors and vulnerabilities before actual exploitation occurs.

Key Tools:

- **Nmap**: A powerful network scanning tool that discovers hosts and services on a network, helping to create a map of the target's infrastructure.
- **Recon-ng:** A full-featured web reconnaissance framework that provides a powerful environment for gathering information about targets.
- **theHarvester**: This tool helps collect emails, subdomains, and other information from various public sources, aiding in the reconnaissance process.

Exploitation Tools

Purpose: Exploitation tools are designed to identify and exploit vulnerabilities in systems, applications, and networks. They enable Red Teams to demonstrate the potential impact of security weaknesses.

Key Tools:

- **Metasploit**: A widely used penetration testing framework that provides a suite of exploits and payloads for various platforms, allowing Red Teams to simulate attacks effectively.
- **Burp Suite**: An integrated platform for performing security testing of web applications, featuring tools for scanning, crawling, and exploiting vulnerabilities.
- **sqlmap**: An open-source penetration testing tool specifically designed for automating the process of detecting and exploiting SQL injection vulnerabilities.

Post-Exploitation Tools

Purpose: After gaining access to a target system, Red Teams use post-exploitation tools to maintain access, gather sensitive information, and evaluate the overall impact of their actions.

Key Tools:

- **Empire**: A PowerShell and Python post-exploitation agent that provides a range of features for maintaining persistence, credential harvesting, and lateral movement within a compromised network.
- **Cobalt Strike**: A commercial tool that offers advanced post-exploitation capabilities, including social engineering features, command-and-control (C2) infrastructure, and evasion techniques.
- **Mimikatz**: A powerful tool used to extract plaintext passwords, hashes, and Kerberos tickets from memory, enabling Red Teams to escalate privileges and move laterally within a network.

Social Engineering Tools

Purpose: Social engineering tools help simulate attacks that exploit human psychology, aiming to manipulate individuals into divulging confidential information or performing actions that compromise security.

Key Tools:

- **Social-Engineer Toolkit (SET):** A framework designed for social engineering penetration testing, allowing Red Teams to craft phishing attacks, credential harvesters, and other social engineering tactics.
- **Gophish**: An open-source phishing framework that enables Red Teams to create and manage phishing campaigns, track user interactions, and assess the effectiveness of training initiatives.
- **PhishX**: A tool for simulating phishing attacks and providing analytics on user responses, helping organizations improve their security awareness training.

Physical Security Testing Tools

Purpose: Physical security testing tools are used to assess the physical security controls of an organization, including access controls, surveillance systems, and environmental security measures.

Key Tools:

- **RFID Cloning Tools**: Devices designed to clone RFID credentials, allowing Red Teams to test the effectiveness of access control systems.
- **Lock Picking Sets**: Tools used to test physical locks and assess the robustness of physical security measures in place at a facility.
- **Camera and Surveillance Testing Tools**: Devices that can assess the coverage and effectiveness of surveillance systems, ensuring that all entry points are monitored adequately.

Reporting and Collaboration Tools

Purpose: Reporting and collaboration tools help Red Teams document their findings, communicate with stakeholders, and create actionable reports that inform security improvements.

Key Tools:

- **Dradis**: An open-source collaboration and reporting framework that helps teams organize their findings, manage tasks, and generate comprehensive reports.
- **Faraday**: An integrated multi-user pentest environment that centralizes data collection, analysis, and reporting, allowing for streamlined collaboration among team members.
- **ReportGenerator**: A tool that automates the process of generating professional reports from multiple sources, ensuring that findings are presented clearly and concisely.

Selecting the Right Tools

Choosing the right tools for Red Team operations involves several considerations:

Scope of Engagement: The tools selected should align with the specific objectives and scope of the Red Team engagement. For instance, if the focus is on web application testing, tools like Burp Suite and sqlmap would be more relevant.

Team Expertise: Consider the skill sets and expertise of the team members. Utilizing tools that the team is familiar with can enhance efficiency and effectiveness during engagements.

Integration and Compatibility: Assess the compatibility of tools with existing security tools and processes within the organization. Tools that integrate seamlessly with other systems can streamline workflows and improve overall effectiveness.

Cost and Licensing: Evaluate the costs associated with tools, especially commercial solutions. Open-source tools can be cost-effective alternatives but may require additional investment in training and support.

Community Support and Documentation: Tools with robust community support and comprehensive documentation are often easier to implement and troubleshoot. Engaging with user communities can also provide valuable insights and best practices.

Essential Red Team tools are critical for conducting effective assessments and simulating real-world attacks. By utilizing a diverse array of tools across various categories, Red Teams can gather intelligence, exploit vulnerabilities, maintain access, and report findings comprehensively. Selecting the right tools based on the engagement scope, team expertise, and organizational needs ensures that Red Teams can effectively identify weaknesses and provide actionable recommendations for improving security posture. As the cybersecurity landscape continues to evolve, staying updated on new tools and methodologies is vital for Red Teams to maintain their effectiveness in defending against emerging threats.

13.2 Comparison of Open Source vs. Commercial Tools

When it comes to Red Team operations, selecting the right tools is crucial for success. The cybersecurity community offers a wide range of tools, broadly categorized into two types: open-source tools and commercial tools. Both types have their own advantages and disadvantages, and the choice between them often depends on the specific needs, budget constraints, and expertise of the Red Team. This section provides a comprehensive comparison of open-source and commercial tools, examining their features, benefits, and limitations.

Open Source Tools

Definition: Open-source tools are software programs whose source code is publicly available. This allows users to inspect, modify, and distribute the software freely.

Examples:

- **Nmap**: A network scanning tool used to discover hosts and services.
- **Metasploit** Community: An open-source penetration testing framework that enables users to find vulnerabilities in systems.
- **Burp Suite Community Edition**: A limited version of the widely used web application security testing tool.

Advantages:

Cost-Effective: Open-source tools are typically free to use, making them an attractive option for organizations with limited budgets or those just starting their Red Team operations.

Customization and Flexibility: Since the source code is available, users can customize tools to suit their specific needs. This flexibility can lead to the development of unique functionalities that may not be available in commercial products.

Active Community Support: Many open-source tools have active user communities that contribute to the development, improvement, and troubleshooting of the software. This collaborative environment can provide valuable insights and updates.

Transparency: Open-source tools promote transparency since users can review the code for security vulnerabilities, ensuring there are no hidden backdoors or malicious features.

Diversity of Options: The open-source ecosystem is vast, offering a wide variety of tools for different purposes (e.g., reconnaissance, exploitation, reporting), allowing teams to select tools that best fit their workflows.

Disadvantages:

Limited Support: While community support is available, it may not be as comprehensive or responsive as dedicated customer support provided by commercial vendors. Organizations may need to rely on internal expertise for troubleshooting.

Learning Curve: Some open-source tools may require more technical knowledge to set up and use effectively, which could present challenges for less experienced team members.

Inconsistent Quality: The quality and reliability of open-source tools can vary significantly, as they are often developed by volunteers or small teams. This inconsistency may lead to performance issues or bugs.

Documentation Gaps: Although many open-source tools have documentation, it may not always be complete or easy to understand, making it difficult for new users to learn how to use the tools effectively.

Commercial Tools

Definition: Commercial tools are proprietary software products developed and sold by companies. These tools typically come with customer support, regular updates, and additional features.

Examples:

- **Cobalt Strike**: A commercial penetration testing tool designed for advanced Red Team operations, featuring comprehensive post-exploitation capabilities.

- **Burp Suite Professional**: A commercial version of Burp Suite, offering enhanced features for web application security testing.
- **Core Impact**: A comprehensive penetration testing tool that integrates multiple functionalities for assessing security across various environments.

Advantages:

Professional Support: Commercial tools often come with dedicated customer support, providing assistance with installation, configuration, and troubleshooting, which can be invaluable for organizations lacking in-house expertise.

User-Friendly Interfaces: Many commercial tools are designed with user-friendly interfaces that streamline workflows and enhance usability, making them accessible to both experienced and novice users.

Regular Updates and Maintenance: Commercial vendors frequently release updates to address vulnerabilities, add new features, and ensure compatibility with the latest technologies, providing users with reliable tools.

Comprehensive Features: Commercial tools often include a wide range of functionalities, integrations, and reporting capabilities, making them versatile solutions for various Red Team activities.

Training and Resources: Many commercial vendors offer training, documentation, and resources to help users maximize the value of their tools, facilitating a quicker learning curve.

Disadvantages:

Cost: Commercial tools can be expensive, with licensing fees that may strain the budgets of smaller organizations or startups. Ongoing subscription models can also lead to long-term financial commitments.

Vendor Lock-In: Organizations may become dependent on specific commercial tools, making it challenging to switch to alternatives in the future. This dependency can also lead to concerns about ongoing costs and support.

Less Flexibility: Commercial tools may not allow users to modify or customize the software to the same extent as open-source tools, limiting the ability to tailor functionalities to specific needs.

Transparency Issues: The proprietary nature of commercial tools means that users do not have access to the source code. This lack of transparency can raise concerns about security and potential hidden vulnerabilities.

Key Considerations for Tool Selection

When choosing between open-source and commercial tools for Red Team operations, several factors should be considered:

Budget Constraints: Evaluate the organization's budget and determine how much can be allocated to tool procurement. Open-source tools may be the best option for limited budgets.

Skill Level of Team Members: Consider the expertise of the Red Team members. If the team has strong technical skills, open-source tools may be feasible. Conversely, if team members require more guidance, commercial tools may be more suitable.

Specific Use Cases: Assess the specific needs of the Red Team. For certain tasks, such as web application testing, commercial tools like Burp Suite Professional may provide advanced features that justify the cost.

Long-Term Strategy: Consider the organization's long-term strategy regarding cybersecurity investments. Open-source tools may be suitable for short-term engagements, while commercial tools might be better for ongoing assessments.

Integration Needs: Evaluate how well the tools can integrate with existing security infrastructure and workflows. Tools that seamlessly fit into the organization's processes will enhance efficiency and effectiveness.

Both open-source and commercial tools play vital roles in the Red Team toolkit, each offering unique benefits and challenges. Open-source tools provide cost-effective solutions with flexibility and customization, while commercial tools deliver robust support, user-friendly interfaces, and comprehensive features. The choice between the two ultimately depends on the organization's specific needs, budget, and the expertise of the Red Team. A balanced approach that leverages both types of tools may also be beneficial, allowing organizations to maximize their effectiveness in identifying and addressing security vulnerabilities. As the cybersecurity landscape continues to evolve, staying informed about the latest tools and technologies will be essential for Red Teams to maintain their effectiveness and adapt to emerging threats.

13.3 Setting Up a Red Team Lab

A well-equipped Red Team lab is essential for conducting effective penetration testing and security assessments. It provides a controlled environment where Red Team members can hone their skills, test various tools and techniques, and simulate real-world attack scenarios without risking harm to live systems. This section outlines the steps and considerations involved in setting up a Red Team lab, including hardware and software requirements, network configuration, and best practices for ensuring a productive and secure testing environment.

1. Defining Lab Objectives

Before diving into the technical aspects of setting up a lab, it is crucial to define its objectives. The purpose of the lab will guide decisions regarding hardware, software, and network configurations. Some common objectives include:

- **Skill Development**: Providing a space for team members to practice and improve their technical skills in penetration testing, exploitation, and threat simulation.
- **Tool Testing**: Evaluating new tools and methodologies before deploying them in real-world engagements.
- **Scenario Simulation**: Creating realistic attack scenarios to assess the effectiveness of existing security controls and incident response procedures.
- **Team Collaboration**: Facilitating collaboration and communication among team members during training exercises and assessments.

2. Hardware Requirements

Setting up a Red Team lab requires a variety of hardware components. The specific requirements will depend on the lab's objectives, but essential components typically include:

Workstations: Each team member should have a dedicated workstation equipped with sufficient processing power, RAM, and storage to run multiple virtual machines (VMs) and tools. A recommended configuration includes:

- At least 16GB of RAM
- Multi-core CPU (e.g., Intel i5/i7 or AMD Ryzen)

- SSD storage for faster performance

Servers: If the lab requires centralized services, consider deploying servers to host applications, databases, or other infrastructure components. This can be done using dedicated physical servers or cloud-based solutions.

Networking Equipment: A reliable network infrastructure is crucial for testing communication between VMs and real devices. Essential equipment includes:

- Routers and switches to create a local area network (LAN)
- Firewalls to control traffic flow and simulate real-world security measures
- Wireless access points if wireless testing is part of the lab's objectives

3. Software Requirements

The choice of software will depend on the tools and platforms needed for the lab. Key categories of software include:

Operating Systems: Install multiple operating systems to simulate different environments and target systems. Common choices include:

- **Windows**: Use various versions (e.g., Windows 10, Windows Server) to test exploits and attacks specific to Microsoft environments.
- **Linux**: Distributions such as Kali Linux, Parrot Security OS, and Ubuntu can be used for penetration testing and security assessments.

Virtualization Software: Use platforms like VMware, VirtualBox, or Hyper-V to create and manage multiple VMs, allowing for easy snapshots and configurations.

Penetration Testing Tools: Install a comprehensive suite of tools for various stages of Red Team operations, including:

- **Reconnaissance**: Nmap, Recon-ng, theHarvester
- **Exploitation**: Metasploit, Burp Suite, sqlmap
- **Post-Exploitation**: Empire, Cobalt Strike, Mimikatz
- **Social Engineering**: SET, Gophish, PhishX

Collaboration and Reporting Tools: Implement tools for documentation, reporting, and team collaboration, such as Dradis, Faraday, and JIRA.

4. Network Configuration

A well-designed network layout is essential for a Red Team lab to facilitate realistic testing. Key considerations include:

- **Isolation**: Ensure the lab network is isolated from the organization's production environment to prevent any unintended impact on live systems. This can be achieved using VLANs or dedicated physical networks.
- **Network Segmentation**: Create separate segments within the lab for different purposes, such as a segment for attack simulations, one for target systems, and another for command-and-control (C2) infrastructure. This allows for better control and monitoring of traffic.
- **Firewall Rules**: Implement firewall rules to control access between different segments and simulate real-world security controls. This helps in testing how well defenses stand up against various attack vectors.
- **VPN Access**: If remote access is necessary, consider setting up a secure Virtual Private Network (VPN) for team members to connect to the lab securely.

5. Best Practices for Lab Setup

To ensure the effectiveness of the Red Team lab, consider the following best practices:

- **Regular Updates**: Keep all software, tools, and operating systems updated to mitigate vulnerabilities and improve the overall security posture of the lab environment.
- **Backup and Recovery**: Implement a robust backup and recovery plan to protect data and configurations. Regularly create snapshots of VMs to allow easy restoration to a previous state in case of failures or misconfigurations.
- **Documentation**: Maintain comprehensive documentation of the lab's architecture, configurations, and procedures. This will facilitate onboarding new team members and ensure continuity in operations.
- **Testing Scenarios**: Develop a library of predefined testing scenarios that can be executed in the lab. This will provide structure to training sessions and ensure that team members are exposed to various attack techniques and methodologies.
- **Continuous Learning**: Encourage team members to engage in continuous learning by attending workshops, online courses, and conferences related to cybersecurity. Staying updated on emerging threats and techniques will enhance the overall effectiveness of the Red Team.

6. Evaluation and Improvement

Once the lab is operational, it is essential to regularly evaluate its effectiveness. Collect feedback from team members on the lab's usability, the relevance of tools, and the realism of simulated scenarios. Use this feedback to make iterative improvements to the lab setup and ensure it remains a valuable resource for Red Team operations.

Setting up a Red Team lab is a critical investment in developing and maintaining a skilled security team capable of identifying and addressing vulnerabilities in an organization's systems. By defining clear objectives, selecting appropriate hardware and software, configuring the network correctly, and following best practices, organizations can create a robust lab environment that fosters skill development, collaboration, and continuous improvement. As the cybersecurity landscape evolves, maintaining an effective Red Team lab will be essential for staying ahead of emerging threats and enhancing overall security posture.

Chapter 14: Real-World Red Team Engagements

In this chapter, we delve into the practical applications of red teaming by examining real-world engagements that illustrate the impact and effectiveness of these operations. Through a series of detailed case studies, we will analyze both successful and unsuccessful red team exercises, highlighting the methodologies employed, the challenges faced, and the outcomes achieved. Each case study will provide valuable insights into the tactics used by red teams and the lessons learned by organizations in response to these simulated attacks. We will also discuss how different organizations approached red teaming, including their objectives, scope, and how they integrated findings into their security strategies. Furthermore, this chapter will highlight common pitfalls and mistakes encountered during red team engagements, offering guidance on how to avoid these issues in future operations. By the end of this chapter, readers will gain a deeper understanding of the real-world implications of red teaming, empowering them to appreciate its value in identifying vulnerabilities and reinforcing the need for a proactive security approach. This exploration will reinforce the idea that red teaming is not just about testing defenses, but also about fostering a culture of resilience and continuous improvement within organizations.

14.1 Case Studies of Successful Red Team Operations

Red Team operations are critical for organizations seeking to bolster their cybersecurity posture. Through simulated attacks, Red Teams can identify vulnerabilities, test incident response plans, and provide valuable insights that help improve overall security. This section explores notable case studies of successful Red Team operations, highlighting key objectives, methodologies, findings, and lessons learned from each engagement.

Case Study 1: Financial Institution Penetration Test

Objective: A large financial institution engaged a Red Team to assess its security posture against advanced persistent threats (APTs). The aim was to identify weaknesses in their network infrastructure, applications, and employee awareness regarding social engineering attacks.

Methodology:

- **Reconnaissance**: The team gathered open-source intelligence (OSINT) about the organization, identifying key personnel, email addresses, and potential attack vectors.
- **Social Engineering**: The Red Team conducted a phishing campaign targeting employees to gauge their susceptibility to social engineering attacks.
- **Exploitation**: After gaining initial access through successful phishing, the team leveraged this foothold to conduct lateral movement within the network, exploiting vulnerabilities in various applications.

Findings:

- The Red Team successfully breached the organization's internal network within hours, demonstrating the effectiveness of the phishing attack.
- They identified critical vulnerabilities in web applications that could lead to data exfiltration and unauthorized access to sensitive financial information.
- Employee awareness training was found to be insufficient, as many employees fell victim to social engineering attempts.

Lessons Learned:

- The financial institution implemented mandatory security awareness training for all employees, emphasizing the importance of recognizing phishing attempts.
- They adopted a continuous security monitoring strategy to detect and respond to potential threats more effectively.
- Regular penetration testing was scheduled to ensure the security measures remained robust against evolving attack techniques.

Case Study 2: Healthcare Provider Security Assessment

Objective: A regional healthcare provider wanted to evaluate its cybersecurity defenses, particularly regarding patient data protection and compliance with regulations like HIPAA.

Methodology:

- **Network Scanning**: The Red Team conducted thorough network scans to identify open ports, services, and outdated software versions.
- **Physical Security Testing**: The team attempted to gain physical access to facilities to assess security measures and potential vulnerabilities in visitor management.

- **Post-Exploitation**: After gaining access to the network, the Red Team tested data exfiltration techniques to evaluate the effectiveness of data loss prevention (DLP) measures.

Findings:

- The assessment revealed several outdated software versions, including a critical vulnerability in the electronic health record (EHR) system.
- The Red Team successfully gained physical access to sensitive areas of the facility due to inadequate badge access controls and security personnel awareness.
- Data exfiltration tests demonstrated that sensitive patient information could be extracted without triggering alarms or alerts.

Lessons Learned:

- The healthcare provider prioritized software updates and patch management to address identified vulnerabilities.
- They enhanced physical security measures by improving visitor management processes and conducting staff training on recognizing suspicious behavior.
- Regular DLP assessments were scheduled to ensure ongoing compliance with data protection regulations.

Case Study 3: Government Agency Cybersecurity Assessment

Objective: A government agency sought to assess its cybersecurity posture in light of increasing cyber threats from nation-state actors. The goal was to evaluate the resilience of its critical infrastructure systems.

Methodology:

- **Threat Modeling**: The Red Team conducted threat modeling to understand the specific risks facing the agency, focusing on critical infrastructure components.
- **Advanced Attack Simulations**: Utilizing advanced tactics, techniques, and procedures (TTPs) used by nation-state actors, the team executed a series of simulated attacks.
- **Incident Response Testing**: The agency's incident response team was engaged during the operation to test their ability to detect and respond to real-time threats.

Findings:

- The Red Team successfully infiltrated several critical systems, gaining access to sensitive information that could be leveraged in a real-world attack scenario.
- The agency's incident response team struggled to identify and contain the simulated threats, leading to a delayed response.
- The Red Team's tactics highlighted weaknesses in both technology and personnel preparedness.

Lessons Learned:

- The government agency implemented an enhanced incident response training program to improve team readiness and effectiveness.
- They conducted tabletop exercises to simulate cyber incidents and refine response protocols.
- The agency committed to regular Red Team assessments to ensure the ongoing resilience of critical infrastructure systems.

Case Study 4: Retail Company Security Evaluation

Objective: A major retail company sought to evaluate its cybersecurity posture following a series of high-profile breaches in the industry. The goal was to assess its defenses against credit card fraud and data theft.

Methodology:

- **Vulnerability Assessment**: The Red Team conducted a comprehensive vulnerability assessment of the retail company's e-commerce platform and point-of-sale (POS) systems.
- **Simulated Attacks**: Using techniques commonly employed by attackers, the team simulated attacks to exploit identified vulnerabilities.
- **Social Engineering and Phishing**: The team also executed a social engineering campaign targeting employees with access to sensitive customer data.

Findings:

- The Red Team identified critical vulnerabilities in the e-commerce platform that could be exploited to steal customer credit card information.
- Successful social engineering attempts led to compromised employee accounts, allowing further access to sensitive data.

- The POS systems were found to be inadequately protected against certain types of attacks.

Lessons Learned:

- The retail company invested in enhancing its application security practices, including code reviews and regular penetration testing of its e-commerce platform.
- They implemented stricter access controls and authentication measures for employees handling sensitive data.
- Continuous training and awareness programs were established to strengthen the organization's defenses against social engineering attacks.

These case studies illustrate the diverse applications and benefits of Red Team operations across various industries. Through real-world simulations and targeted assessments, organizations can identify vulnerabilities, strengthen defenses, and improve incident response capabilities. The insights gained from these engagements lead to practical changes that significantly enhance an organization's overall security posture. As cyber threats continue to evolve, the importance of Red Team operations in proactively addressing vulnerabilities cannot be overstated. By learning from successful Red Team engagements, organizations can better prepare themselves against an ever-changing threat landscape.

14.2 Common Pitfalls and How to Avoid Them

Red Team operations are essential for identifying vulnerabilities and testing an organization's security posture. However, several common pitfalls can hinder the effectiveness of these operations. Understanding these pitfalls and knowing how to avoid them can significantly enhance the outcomes of Red Team engagements. This section outlines some of the most frequent challenges encountered in Red Team operations and offers practical strategies for mitigating these risks.

1. Lack of Clear Objectives

Pitfall: One of the most significant pitfalls in Red Team operations is the absence of clear objectives and success criteria. Without defined goals, Red Teams may conduct assessments that do not align with organizational needs, leading to unclear outcomes and wasted resources.

How to Avoid:

- **Define Clear Objectives**: Before commencing any engagement, stakeholders should collaborate to outline specific goals. This may include identifying critical assets, potential attack vectors, and the desired level of risk assessment.
- **Establish Success Criteria**: Create measurable success criteria to evaluate the effectiveness of the Red Team's operations. This could include metrics like the time taken to breach specific systems or the effectiveness of existing security controls.

2. Inadequate Scoping

Pitfall: Poorly defined scope can lead to engagement failures, where the Red Team either overreaches or under-delivers. A lack of clarity on what is included in the assessment can result in significant blind spots or wasted efforts.

How to Avoid:

- **Conduct a Thorough Scoping Exercise**: Collaborate with stakeholders to define the boundaries of the engagement. Identify which systems, applications, and environments will be included and which will be excluded.
- **Adjust Scope Based on Findings**: Be prepared to adapt the scope during the engagement based on initial findings. If new vulnerabilities are discovered, discuss with stakeholders whether to explore those areas further.

3. Insufficient Communication

Pitfall: Ineffective communication between the Red Team and organizational stakeholders can lead to misunderstandings and misaligned expectations. This can result in delayed responses, a lack of support during engagements, and unaddressed findings.

How to Avoid:

- **Establish Regular Communication Channels**: Set up regular meetings or status updates to ensure all parties are aligned throughout the engagement. This helps maintain transparency and fosters collaboration.
- **Create a Reporting Framework**: Develop a structured reporting process that includes interim findings and post-engagement debriefs. This ensures that stakeholders receive timely updates and can act on critical issues promptly.

4. Neglecting Legal and Ethical Considerations

Pitfall: Red Team operations can inadvertently breach legal and ethical boundaries, particularly regarding data privacy and access permissions. Ignoring these aspects can lead to legal repercussions and damage the organization's reputation.

How to Avoid:

- **Establish Legal Frameworks**: Collaborate with legal teams to develop clear agreements outlining the parameters of the engagement. This should include consent from the organization and any third parties that may be impacted.
- **Develop Ethical Guidelines**: Create and enforce ethical guidelines that govern Red Team operations. Ensure that all team members understand and adhere to these standards throughout the engagement.

5. Overlooking Post-Engagement Activities

Pitfall: Organizations often focus heavily on the technical aspects of Red Team operations while neglecting the importance of post-engagement activities, such as reporting, debriefing, and follow-up actions.

How to Avoid:

- **Implement a Structured Reporting Process**: Ensure that findings are documented comprehensively, highlighting vulnerabilities, attack paths, and recommended remediation strategies. This documentation should be accessible to relevant stakeholders.
- **Conduct Debriefing Sessions**: Organize debriefing sessions with stakeholders to discuss findings and recommendations. This helps to reinforce lessons learned and facilitates the development of action plans to address identified weaknesses.

6. Failing to Integrate Red Teaming into Security Programs

Pitfall: Treating Red Team operations as a one-off exercise rather than an ongoing component of an organization's security strategy can limit their effectiveness. Without integration into broader security initiatives, organizations may fail to leverage insights gained from Red Team engagements.

How to Avoid:

- **Make Red Teaming a Continuous Practice**: Incorporate Red Team operations into the overall security strategy as a regular practice. Schedule periodic assessments to keep security measures up to date.
- **Align Red Team Findings with Security Improvements**: Ensure that the findings from Red Team operations are used to inform security program improvements, such as updating policies, enhancing training, and strengthening technology.

7. Ignoring Team Dynamics and Skills Development

Pitfall: Red Teams can become stagnant if they fail to focus on team dynamics, skills development, and knowledge sharing. This can lead to a lack of innovation and an inability to adapt to new threats.

How to Avoid:

- **Encourage Continuous Learning**: Promote a culture of continuous learning and skill development among Red Team members. Provide opportunities for training, certifications, and participation in cybersecurity conferences.
- **Facilitate Knowledge Sharing**: Encourage team members to share insights and lessons learned from each engagement. This helps build collective knowledge and enhances the team's ability to innovate and adapt.

8. Inadequate Tools and Resources

Pitfall: Insufficient tools and resources can limit the effectiveness of Red Team operations. Relying on outdated tools or lacking access to critical resources can hinder the team's ability to conduct thorough assessments.

How to Avoid:

- **Invest in Tools and Technologies**: Regularly evaluate and invest in the latest tools and technologies relevant to Red Team operations. This includes both open-source and commercial solutions that enhance capabilities.
- **Create a Resource Repository**: Develop a centralized repository of tools, scripts, and resources that team members can access to facilitate their work. This encourages efficiency and consistency in operations.

Red Team operations play a vital role in strengthening an organization's cybersecurity posture. However, by understanding and proactively addressing common pitfalls, organizations can significantly enhance the effectiveness of these operations. By setting clear objectives, maintaining open communication, considering legal and ethical implications, and integrating findings into ongoing security programs, organizations can maximize the benefits of Red Team engagements. Additionally, investing in team dynamics, skills development, and adequate resources ensures that Red Teams remain agile, innovative, and capable of adapting to an ever-evolving threat landscape. Ultimately, avoiding these pitfalls will lead to more successful Red Team operations and a more resilient security posture for the organization as a whole.

14.3 Impact of Red Teaming on Organizational Security Posture

Red Teaming is an essential component of a comprehensive cybersecurity strategy, providing organizations with a simulated adversarial perspective on their security posture. The impact of Red Team operations on organizational security can be profound, influencing various aspects of risk management, incident response, employee awareness, and overall resilience against cyber threats. This section delves into the multifaceted impact of Red Teaming on an organization's security posture and how it contributes to strengthening defenses and improving preparedness.

1. Identification of Vulnerabilities

Enhanced Vulnerability Discovery: One of the primary impacts of Red Teaming is the identification of security vulnerabilities that may not be uncovered through traditional security assessments. Red Teams simulate real-world attack scenarios, often employing tactics that automated scanning tools cannot replicate. This leads to the discovery of weaknesses in networks, applications, and processes that might otherwise go unnoticed.

Proactive Risk Management: By identifying vulnerabilities before they can be exploited by actual attackers, organizations can adopt a proactive risk management approach. This enables them to prioritize remediation efforts based on the severity and potential impact of the vulnerabilities identified, ultimately reducing the likelihood of successful attacks.

2. Improvement in Incident Response Capabilities

Testing Incident Response Plans: Red Team operations provide an opportunity to test and evaluate an organization's incident response plans under realistic conditions. By simulating attacks, Red Teams can assess how effectively incident response teams can detect, respond to, and recover from security incidents.

Identifying Gaps in Preparedness: Engagements often reveal gaps in incident response procedures, including weaknesses in detection capabilities, communication protocols, and escalation paths. Organizations can address these gaps, leading to improved readiness for actual security incidents.

3. Strengthening Security Awareness and Culture

Employee Awareness Training: Red Team operations frequently include social engineering tactics, such as phishing simulations, which are designed to test employee awareness. These exercises serve as a wake-up call for employees, highlighting the importance of vigilance and security practices.

Fostering a Security Culture: By involving employees in the Red Team process and emphasizing the importance of security awareness, organizations can foster a security-first culture. Employees become more engaged in protecting sensitive data and are better equipped to recognize and respond to potential threats.

4. Enhanced Collaboration and Communication

Cross-Departmental Collaboration: Red Team engagements often require collaboration between various departments, including IT, security, and executive leadership. This fosters a culture of communication and teamwork, helping to break down silos that can hinder effective security practices.

Executive Buy-In: Engaging executives in the Red Team process and sharing findings can lead to increased support for security initiatives and funding for necessary improvements. When leadership understands the potential risks and vulnerabilities revealed by Red Team operations, they are more likely to prioritize cybersecurity investments.

5. Validation of Security Controls

Assessing Effectiveness of Controls: Red Teaming provides organizations with the opportunity to validate the effectiveness of existing security controls. By attempting to bypass these controls through simulated attacks, organizations can assess whether their defenses are functioning as intended.

Continuous Improvement: The insights gained from Red Team engagements can inform continuous improvement initiatives, prompting organizations to update policies, strengthen technical controls, and enhance overall security measures based on real-world scenarios.

6. Compliance and Regulatory Benefits

Meeting Compliance Requirements: Many industries are subject to regulatory requirements regarding data protection and cybersecurity. Regular Red Team assessments can help organizations demonstrate compliance with these requirements by providing documented evidence of proactive security measures and vulnerability assessments.

Building Trust with Stakeholders: By taking proactive steps to identify and remediate vulnerabilities, organizations can build trust with stakeholders, including customers, partners, and regulators. Demonstrating a commitment to security through Red Team operations can enhance an organization's reputation and competitive advantage.

7. Resilience Against Evolving Threats

Adapting to New Threats: The cyber threat landscape is constantly evolving, with attackers employing increasingly sophisticated tactics. Red Teaming enables organizations to stay ahead of emerging threats by simulating advanced attack scenarios and assessing the effectiveness of defenses against these new tactics.

Strengthening Overall Security Posture: By regularly conducting Red Team engagements, organizations can create a feedback loop that informs their security strategy. Continuous assessments lead to a more resilient security posture, reducing the likelihood of successful attacks and minimizing the impact of incidents when they do occur.

8. Cost-Effective Risk Management

Reducing Incident Costs: By identifying and remediating vulnerabilities before they are exploited, organizations can significantly reduce the potential costs associated with data breaches and security incidents. This includes costs related to incident response, regulatory fines, reputational damage, and customer loss.

Prioritizing Investments: Red Team findings can guide organizations in prioritizing their security investments. By focusing on high-risk areas identified during engagements, organizations can allocate resources more effectively, maximizing their return on investment in security measures.

The impact of Red Teaming on an organization's security posture is profound and far-reaching. By identifying vulnerabilities, improving incident response capabilities, strengthening employee awareness, and fostering collaboration, Red Team operations play a critical role in enhancing overall security. As organizations navigate an increasingly complex cyber threat landscape, the insights gained from Red Team engagements provide valuable guidance for continuous improvement, compliance, and risk management. Ultimately, investing in Red Teaming is not just about uncovering weaknesses; it is about building a resilient security posture that can adapt to evolving threats and safeguard sensitive information.

Chapter 15: The Future of Red Team Operations

In the final chapter, we explore the evolving landscape of red team operations and the factors shaping its future in the cybersecurity domain. As cyber threats become increasingly sophisticated and organizations face more complex challenges, red teaming must adapt and innovate to remain effective. We will begin by examining emerging trends in cybersecurity, such as the rise of artificial intelligence and machine learning, and how these technologies can enhance red team methodologies and automation. Next, we will discuss the growing importance of integrating red teaming with blue team defenses, emphasizing the need for collaboration between offensive and defensive security measures to create a more resilient security posture. The chapter will also explore the impact of regulatory changes and compliance requirements on red team operations, as organizations strive to align their security practices with industry standards. Additionally, we will consider the role of continuous learning and professional development within red teams, highlighting the importance of staying current with evolving tactics and techniques. By the end of this chapter, readers will be equipped with insights into the future direction of red team operations, encouraging them to think proactively about how to adapt and enhance their own security strategies in an ever-changing threat landscape.

15.1 Emerging Trends and Technologies in Red Teaming

As the cybersecurity landscape continues to evolve, so do the methods and tools employed by Red Teams. Emerging trends and technologies are reshaping how Red Teams operate, enabling them to simulate attacks more effectively and assess an organization's security posture comprehensively. This section explores some of the most significant emerging trends and technologies in Red Teaming, highlighting their implications for organizations looking to enhance their cybersecurity defenses.

1. Automation and Orchestration

Overview: The increasing complexity and scale of cyber threats have prompted Red Teams to leverage automation and orchestration tools to streamline their operations. Automation allows Red Teams to perform repetitive tasks efficiently, while orchestration enables seamless integration between various security tools and processes.

Implications:

- **Efficiency Gains**: By automating routine tasks such as reconnaissance and vulnerability scanning, Red Teams can focus on more sophisticated attack scenarios that require human creativity and strategic thinking.
- **Consistent Execution**: Automation ensures that Red Team engagements are executed consistently, reducing the risk of human error and improving the reliability of findings.

2. Artificial Intelligence and Machine Learning

Overview: Artificial Intelligence (AI) and Machine Learning (ML) are gaining traction in Red Team operations. These technologies can analyze vast amounts of data, recognize patterns, and adapt to evolving tactics, making them valuable for simulating advanced attack strategies.

Implications:

- **Adaptive Attack Simulations**: AI and ML can be used to develop adaptive attack simulations that mimic the behavior of sophisticated threat actors. This enables Red Teams to test defenses against more realistic scenarios.
- **Intelligent Reconnaissance**: Machine learning algorithms can analyze large datasets to identify potential vulnerabilities and targets more effectively, improving the reconnaissance phase of Red Team engagements.

3. Cloud Security Testing

Overview: As organizations increasingly migrate to the cloud, Red Teams must adapt their methodologies to assess cloud environments effectively. This includes understanding the unique security challenges posed by cloud services and architecture.

Implications:

- **Focus on Cloud Vulnerabilities**: Red Teams are developing expertise in identifying vulnerabilities specific to cloud configurations, such as misconfigured storage buckets or insecure APIs.
- **Integration of Cloud Tools**: New tools and frameworks specifically designed for cloud security testing are emerging, allowing Red Teams to conduct assessments that account for the complexities of cloud environments.

4. Red Teaming as a Service (RaaS)

Overview: The concept of Red Teaming as a Service (RaaS) is gaining popularity, allowing organizations to outsource their Red Team operations to specialized providers. This trend is particularly beneficial for smaller organizations that may lack the resources to maintain an in-house Red Team.

Implications:

- **Access to Expertise**: Organizations can leverage the expertise of external Red Team providers who bring diverse experience and knowledge of the latest attack trends and technologies.
- **Cost-Effectiveness**: Outsourcing Red Team operations can be a cost-effective solution, allowing organizations to conduct regular assessments without the overhead of maintaining a full-time team.

5. Increased Focus on Social Engineering

Overview: Social engineering remains a critical component of Red Team operations, as human behavior often represents the weakest link in cybersecurity. Emerging trends emphasize the need for comprehensive social engineering testing to assess employee awareness and resilience.

Implications:

- **Innovative Techniques**: Red Teams are adopting new social engineering techniques, such as deepfake technology and advanced phishing simulations, to test the effectiveness of security training programs.
- **Tailored Awareness Training**: Insights from social engineering engagements can inform tailored training programs that address specific weaknesses identified within the organization.

6. Collaboration and Integration with Blue Teams

Overview: The shift toward collaborative security practices is gaining momentum, with Red Teams increasingly working alongside Blue Teams (defensive security teams) to enhance overall security posture. This collaborative approach fosters a culture of continuous improvement.

Implications:

- **Enhanced Learning Opportunities**: By collaborating with Blue Teams, Red Teams can provide valuable insights into the effectiveness of defensive measures, leading to improvements in both offensive and defensive strategies.
- **Joint Exercises**: Conducting joint exercises between Red and Blue Teams allows for real-time learning and adaptation, enabling both teams to refine their techniques and enhance their preparedness.

7. Advanced Tools and Frameworks

Overview: The development of new tools and frameworks continues to shape Red Team operations. Emerging tools leverage automation, AI, and other technologies to enhance the efficiency and effectiveness of Red Team engagements.

Implications:

- **Integration of Open-Source Tools**: A growing number of open-source tools are being developed for Red Teaming, providing organizations with cost-effective solutions to enhance their testing capabilities.
- **Standardized Frameworks**: New frameworks are emerging to standardize Red Team methodologies, making it easier for organizations to align their practices with industry best standards.

8. Focus on Regulatory Compliance

Overview: With increasing regulatory scrutiny in various industries, Red Teams are placing greater emphasis on compliance testing. Organizations must ensure that their security practices align with regulatory requirements, and Red Teams can help identify gaps.

Implications:

- **Compliance Assessments**: Red Teams are incorporating compliance assessments into their engagements to help organizations identify vulnerabilities that may expose them to regulatory risks.
- **Documentation and Reporting**: The focus on compliance necessitates comprehensive documentation and reporting of findings, which can aid organizations in demonstrating compliance to regulators.

9. Continuous Testing and Assessment

Overview: The traditional approach of conducting periodic Red Team engagements is evolving into a model of continuous testing and assessment. This approach allows organizations to remain vigilant against emerging threats.

Implications:

- **Ongoing Vulnerability Discovery**: Continuous testing enables organizations to identify vulnerabilities as they arise, rather than waiting for scheduled assessments. This proactive approach enhances overall security.
- **Integration with DevSecOps**: The integration of Red Teaming into DevSecOps practices ensures that security testing becomes an integral part of the software development lifecycle, improving the security of applications from the outset.

Emerging trends and technologies in Red Teaming are transforming the way organizations assess and enhance their security posture. By leveraging automation, AI, cloud testing, and collaborative practices, Red Teams can provide valuable insights that drive continuous improvement in cybersecurity. As organizations face an ever-evolving threat landscape, staying abreast of these trends is crucial for maintaining a resilient security posture and effectively defending against sophisticated attacks. Embracing these innovations will not only strengthen defenses but also foster a culture of proactive risk management and security awareness within organizations.

15.2 The Role of AI and Automation in Red Team Operations

In the rapidly evolving field of cybersecurity, the integration of Artificial Intelligence (AI) and automation into Red Team operations is revolutionizing the way security assessments are conducted. By enhancing efficiency, improving the accuracy of assessments, and enabling more sophisticated attack simulations, these technologies are transforming Red Teaming into a more agile and proactive practice. This section explores the pivotal role of AI and automation in Red Team operations, examining their benefits, applications, and potential challenges.

1. Enhancing Efficiency and Scalability

Automating Routine Tasks: Red Team operations often involve repetitive tasks such as reconnaissance, vulnerability scanning, and data collection. Automation allows these tasks to be executed faster and with greater accuracy. Tools can be programmed to conduct scans, gather intelligence, and even simulate attacks without direct human intervention.

Time Savings: By automating mundane tasks, Red Teams can focus their efforts on more complex scenarios that require strategic thinking and creativity. This results in significant time savings, allowing teams to conduct more assessments in a shorter time frame.

Scalability: As organizations grow, their attack surfaces expand. Automated tools can scale up efforts to cover larger environments, ensuring comprehensive assessments without a proportional increase in manpower.

2. Intelligent Reconnaissance

Leveraging AI for Data Analysis: AI algorithms can process vast amounts of data during the reconnaissance phase, identifying potential targets and vulnerabilities more effectively than traditional methods. Machine learning models can analyze patterns in historical data to predict potential weaknesses in an organization's defenses.

Enhanced Target Selection: By utilizing AI for target selection, Red Teams can prioritize assets that are most critical to the organization, allowing for more efficient use of resources and increasing the impact of the engagement.

OSINT Gathering: AI-driven tools can automate Open Source Intelligence (OSINT) gathering, scanning public resources, social media, and dark web forums for information related to potential vulnerabilities, attack vectors, and threat actor behavior.

3. Advanced Threat Simulations

Simulating Realistic Attack Scenarios: AI technologies enable Red Teams to simulate advanced and realistic attack scenarios that mimic the behavior of sophisticated threat actors. This includes the use of AI-generated attack patterns that adapt to the organization's defenses in real-time.

Behavioral Mimicking: AI can analyze the tactics, techniques, and procedures (TTPs) of real-world attackers, allowing Red Teams to replicate these behaviors during assessments. This leads to more effective testing of defenses against evolving threats.

Adversarial AI: As attackers increasingly use AI in their strategies, Red Teams must do the same. Adversarial AI can help simulate AI-based attacks, testing how well an organization's defenses can handle such sophisticated techniques.

4. Continuous Testing and Monitoring

Integrating Automation into Continuous Testing: The shift toward continuous security testing is facilitated by automation. Automated tools can regularly assess an organization's security posture, identifying vulnerabilities and weaknesses as they arise.

Real-Time Monitoring: Continuous testing provides organizations with real-time insights into their security posture, allowing for swift remediation of identified vulnerabilities. This proactive approach reduces the risk of successful attacks.

Integration with DevSecOps: Automation in Red Team operations aligns with DevSecOps practices, where security testing is integrated throughout the software development lifecycle. This ensures that applications are assessed for vulnerabilities continuously, rather than waiting for periodic assessments.

5. Improved Vulnerability Discovery

Leveraging Machine Learning for Vulnerability Identification: Machine learning algorithms can analyze software and system behavior to identify potential vulnerabilities. This capability enhances the vulnerability discovery process, allowing Red Teams to focus on high-impact areas.

Predictive Analysis: Machine learning models can be trained on historical vulnerability data, enabling Red Teams to predict areas of weakness based on trends and patterns. This predictive analysis can guide testing efforts more effectively.

Automated Exploit Development: AI can assist in developing exploits for identified vulnerabilities, allowing Red Teams to simulate real-world attacks and test the effectiveness of defenses more thoroughly.

6. Enhanced Reporting and Communication

Streamlining Reporting Processes: The use of AI can also improve the reporting and communication processes associated with Red Team engagements. Automated reporting tools can generate detailed findings and recommendations based on the results of assessments.

Data Visualization: AI-driven data visualization tools can help present complex findings in an easily understandable format, making it simpler for stakeholders to grasp the implications of Red Team findings.

Customized Reporting: AI can tailor reports to different audiences (technical vs. non-technical stakeholders), ensuring that the most relevant information is communicated effectively to each group.

7. Addressing Challenges and Ethical Considerations

Potential Risks of Automation: While AI and automation offer numerous benefits, they also come with challenges. Over-reliance on automated tools may lead to complacency among Red Team members, as automated systems cannot fully replicate the intuition and creativity of human analysts.

Maintaining Human Oversight: It is crucial for Red Teams to maintain a balance between automation and human expertise. Human oversight is necessary to interpret results, make strategic decisions, and adapt to unforeseen circumstances during engagements.

Ethical Considerations: The use of AI in Red Teaming raises ethical questions regarding privacy, consent, and potential misuse of technology. Organizations must establish clear guidelines and ethical frameworks to ensure responsible use of AI tools in cybersecurity.

AI and automation are transforming Red Team operations, enhancing efficiency, improving vulnerability discovery, and enabling more sophisticated threat simulations. By leveraging these technologies, Red Teams can conduct comprehensive assessments, stay ahead of emerging threats, and provide valuable insights that enhance an organization's overall security posture. However, organizations must remain vigilant in addressing the challenges and ethical considerations associated with these advancements. By striking the right balance between technology and human expertise, Red Teams can leverage AI and automation to create a more proactive and resilient cybersecurity strategy, ultimately leading to stronger defenses against cyber threats.

15.3 Predictions for the Future of Cybersecurity

The cybersecurity landscape is in a constant state of evolution, driven by advancements in technology, changes in the threat environment, and the growing sophistication of cyber adversaries. As we look ahead, several key predictions can be made regarding the future of cybersecurity, especially in the context of Red Team operations and broader security strategies. These predictions reflect the trends and challenges organizations will face as they work to protect their assets and information.

1. Increased Integration of Artificial Intelligence

Overview: As AI technologies continue to mature, their integration into cybersecurity practices will become even more pronounced. Organizations will increasingly leverage AI for threat detection, response, and mitigation.

Predictions:

- **Enhanced Threat Detection**: AI and machine learning algorithms will play a critical role in identifying anomalies and potential threats in real time. This will allow organizations to respond more swiftly to emerging threats.
- **Automated Incident Response**: AI will enable automated incident response capabilities, reducing the time it takes to contain and remediate security incidents. As AI tools become more sophisticated, they will learn from past incidents to improve their response strategies.

2. Proliferation of Cybersecurity Regulations

Overview: Governments and regulatory bodies are likely to impose stricter cybersecurity regulations as cyber threats grow in complexity and impact. Organizations will need to adapt to a rapidly changing regulatory environment.

Predictions:

- **Increased Compliance Requirements**: Organizations across various industries will face heightened compliance requirements, necessitating regular security assessments, risk management practices, and transparency in security measures.
- **Focus on Data Protection**: Regulations will increasingly emphasize data protection, leading organizations to implement stronger data encryption, access controls, and privacy measures to safeguard sensitive information.

3. Rise of Zero Trust Security Models

Overview: The traditional perimeter-based security models are becoming less effective in the face of evolving threats. The adoption of Zero Trust security models will gain momentum as organizations recognize the need for more robust access controls.

Predictions:

- **Verification at Every Level**: Organizations will implement Zero Trust principles, requiring continuous verification of users and devices, regardless of their location within or outside the network perimeter.
- **Microsegmentation**: The practice of microsegmentation will become more common, allowing organizations to create smaller, isolated network segments to limit lateral movement in the event of a breach.

4. Growth of Managed Security Service Providers (MSSPs)

Overview: As cybersecurity threats continue to escalate, many organizations, particularly smaller ones, will increasingly turn to Managed Security Service Providers (MSSPs) for expertise and support.

Predictions:

- **Access to Advanced Capabilities**: MSSPs will offer access to advanced security technologies and skilled professionals, allowing organizations to enhance their security posture without the overhead of maintaining a full-time internal team.
- **24/7 Monitoring and Response**: Organizations will benefit from round-the-clock monitoring and incident response capabilities, improving their ability to detect and respond to threats in real-time.

5. Increased Focus on Supply Chain Security

Overview: Recent high-profile breaches have highlighted the vulnerabilities present in supply chains. Organizations will prioritize supply chain security to mitigate risks associated with third-party vendors and partners.

Predictions:

- **Rigorous Vendor Assessments**: Organizations will conduct more thorough assessments of their vendors' security practices and require them to adhere to strict cybersecurity standards.
- **Continuous Monitoring of Supply Chain Risks**: Continuous monitoring and risk assessment of supply chain partners will become standard practice, helping organizations to quickly identify and address potential vulnerabilities.

6. Cybersecurity Skills Gap

Overview: The demand for skilled cybersecurity professionals continues to outpace supply, resulting in a significant skills gap in the industry. This trend is likely to persist in the coming years.

Predictions:

- **Increased Investment in Training**: Organizations will invest more in training and upskilling their existing workforce to address the skills gap and ensure they have the necessary expertise to combat emerging threats.
- **Collaboration with Educational Institutions**: Partnerships between organizations and educational institutions will grow, leading to the development of programs designed to prepare the next generation of cybersecurity professionals.

7. Evolution of Ransomware Tactics

Overview: Ransomware attacks have become increasingly prevalent and sophisticated, and this trend is expected to continue as cybercriminals adapt their tactics.

Predictions:

- **Double and Triple Extortion**: Cybercriminals will employ double and triple extortion tactics, threatening not only to encrypt data but also to release sensitive information publicly unless a ransom is paid.
- **Targeting Critical Infrastructure**: Ransomware attacks will increasingly target critical infrastructure, such as healthcare, energy, and transportation systems, raising the stakes and prompting greater government intervention.

8. Integration of Cybersecurity into Business Strategy

Overview: Organizations will recognize that cybersecurity is not just an IT issue but a fundamental component of their overall business strategy.

Predictions:

- **Board-Level Engagement**: Cybersecurity will be prioritized at the board level, with executives and board members actively engaging in discussions about risk management and cybersecurity investments.
- **Alignment with Business Goals**: Organizations will align their cybersecurity strategies with their overall business goals, ensuring that security measures support organizational objectives rather than hinder them.

9. Evolution of Red Teaming Practices

Overview: As cybersecurity threats evolve, Red Teaming practices will also adapt to meet the challenges posed by new attack vectors and tactics.

Predictions:

- **Greater Emphasis on Continuous Red Teaming**: Organizations will shift toward continuous Red Teaming practices, integrating regular assessments into their security posture to identify weaknesses proactively.
- **Collaboration with Blue Teams**: Red Teams will increasingly collaborate with Blue Teams, fostering a culture of continuous improvement and learning. Joint exercises will become more common, enhancing overall security resilience.

The future of cybersecurity is characterized by rapid change, driven by technological advancements, evolving threats, and increased regulatory scrutiny. As organizations navigate this complex landscape, they must remain agile, adopting new strategies and technologies to strengthen their defenses. The predictions outlined above highlight the need for organizations to embrace innovation, prioritize security, and foster collaboration across teams. By staying ahead of emerging trends and challenges, organizations can enhance their resilience against cyber threats and protect their critical assets and information. The journey ahead will require a proactive and strategic approach to cybersecurity, ensuring that organizations are well-equipped to face the challenges of an ever-evolving digital world.

"Red Team Operations: Practical Approaches to Security Testing" serves as an essential guide for cybersecurity professionals seeking to strengthen their organization's defenses against a myriad of evolving cyber threats. This book delves into the art and science of red teaming, providing a practical framework for understanding and implementing effective security testing methodologies.

Through a comprehensive exploration of topics ranging from the foundational concepts of red teaming to advanced exploitation techniques, readers will gain valuable insights into how to think like an attacker. Each chapter is designed to equip readers with the knowledge and tools necessary to identify vulnerabilities, enhance security protocols, and foster a proactive security culture within their organizations.

Key themes explored in the book include:

- **Understanding the Threat Landscape**: An overview of current trends and attack vectors that underline the importance of red teaming.
- **Building and Training a Red Team**: Guidance on the essential skills, roles, and continuous learning required to form a successful red team.
- **Red Team Methodologies**: A review of frameworks and approaches that guide red teaming efforts, ensuring alignment with organizational goals.
- **Practical Engagement Strategies**: Detailed discussions on planning, reconnaissance, exploitation, and post-exploitation tactics that simulate real-world attack scenarios.
- **Effective Communication**: Strategies for reporting findings and conducting debriefings that drive improvements in security posture.
- **Lessons Learned and Continuous Improvement**: Emphasizing the importance of iterative learning and adaptation in an ever-changing cyber landscape.

Through case studies, practical examples, and actionable strategies, this book empowers readers to elevate their security testing efforts and effectively prepare for potential threats. "Red Team Operations" not only emphasizes the significance of red teaming as a crucial component of a comprehensive security strategy but also inspires a culture of resilience and vigilance in the face of cyber adversities.

As the cybersecurity landscape continues to evolve, this book serves as a valuable resource for anyone committed to staying ahead of the curve and building a more secure future.